SHIBLĪ

SHIBLĪ

His Life and Thought in the Sufi Tradition

Kenneth Avery

SUNY
PRESS

Published by State University of New York Press, Albany

Printed in the United States of America

For information, contact State University of New York Press, Albany, NY
www.sunypress.edu

Production by Ryan Morris
Marketing by Anne M. Valentine

Library of Congress Cataloging-in-Publication Data

Avery, Kenneth.
Shiblī : his life and thought in the Sufi tradition / Kenneth Avery.
pages cm
Includes bibliographical references.
ISBN 978-1-4384-5179-4 (hc : alk. paper) 978-1-4384-5180-0 (pb : alk. paper)
1. Shiblī, Abu Bakr, 861-946. 2. Sufis—Biography. 3. Sufism—Doctrines—History. I. Title.
BP80.S5365A94 2014
297.4092—dc23
[B] 2013025959

10 9 8 7 6 5 4 3 2 1

Contents

Acknowledgments

An earlier version of chapter 19, titled "The Question of Shiblī's Insanity," appeared in the journal *Sufi* 79, Summer/Autumn 2010.

An earlier version of chapter 20, titled "The Mystical Poetry of Shiblī," appeared in A-T. Tymieniecka (ed.), *Reason, Spirit and the Sacral in the New Enlightenment*, Springer Science+Business Media B.V., 2011.

Permission to use these copyrighted pieces is gratefully acknowledged.

CHAPTER 1

Introduction

In the second quarter of the tenth century, following the cruel and scandalous execution of the Sufi mystic Manṣūr al-Ḥallāj in Baghdad, a lesser-known man was committed to the insane asylum of that great capital of the Muslim world. The treatment he received, the best available at the time, was little more than crude potions and shackling with chains. During his stay in the asylum he received visitors. "Who are you?" he asked. "We are your friends" came the reply. The man picked up some stones and began to throw them at the visitors. When they fled he shouted after them, "Liars! You claim to be my friends, but you cannot endure my testing!"

That man, Abū Bakr al-Shiblī, was no ordinary person. He was a singular individual of great intensity, spirituality, and perception, of remarkable wit and learning. His illness was, for him, just another stage on his inner journey, his search for the transcendent, for the Reality that lay in and beyond everyday appearance.

But did the events reported in this anecdote really take place? Such stories about Shiblī's life later became the stuff of legend and folktale. They developed their own momentum and their own luxuriant growth, and in the hands of admirers, disciples, and hagiographers they were added to and changed over the centuries.

We know that he was born into a wealthy family, trained as a Mālikī scholar, "converted" to the Sufi path aged about forty, was a disciple of Khayr al-Nassāj and the famed Junayd, led an unconventional life of strict austerities and discipline, with some bouts of mental unbalance, and died in his eighties in 946. But these are only the bare bones of his exceptional life, and we know few other precise details.

While Shiblī became a prime subject for later hagiography, is it possible that we can come to know more about him, to peel away the layers of pious tradition and discover the real facts about his life and thought?

Richard Gramlich writes that Shiblī's historical figure soon disappeared after his death under a luminous, legendary idealization that kept developing through the centuries. The traditional biographical details are nearly all anecdotes of unknown historical basis and detached contexts. Sometimes other important figures merely play an ideological role in these anecdotes, their dialogue or questions to Shiblī serving to place his personality and teaching at the center of the narrative.[1]

Shiblī's figure shines with contrasting colors: a rigorous ascetic and a corpulent man with an enormous showy beard; capable of extreme self-abasement and unbecoming pride; a great traditionist, esteemed Mālikī scholar and Sufi master but at the same time a madman often needing asylum; witty in his speech but foolish in his conduct. What are we to make of him? Even Junayd, the great master of the Baghdad "school" of Sufis, wavered between stern reproach and the highest praise.[2]

Having left no writings, his sayings were transmitted orally and eventually found their place scattered among numerous authors. There was no biographer, but the many anecdotes that found their way into later writings form the basis for our picture of him. Yet, as Gramlich notes, it is not the historical biography that is really preserved, though some historical data are revealed, but the nature of his spiritual and intellectual world.[3]

Why is Shiblī important, and why should we be eager to know his life and sayings? In brief, the answer is that he was an exceptional person, a genuinely spiritual man, a God-centered individual who by example showed the path of intense devotion and the transcendental journey. It is in this way that the various writings that preserve his anecdotes and teachings are not important primarily as historical sources, but as disclosing to later generations the essence of his spirituality, thought, and action.

There are further systematic and genealogical reasons for Shiblī's importance. He is a key figure in the transmission and preservation of the Baghdad "school" of Sufism, usually centering on the "sober" Junayd, but also containing elements of the more unconventional and "intoxicated" mysticism represented by Shiblī. Abū ʿAbd al-Raḥmān al-Sulamī (d. 1021), the most important collector of tradition (*ḥadīth*) and Qurʾān commentary (*tafsīr*) for early

Sufism, was a disciple of Abū ʾl-Qāsim al-Naṣrābādhī (d. 977–978), a disciple of Shiblī. It is thus no accident that Shiblī's is the longest biography in Sulamī's influential collection of Sufi "lives," the *Ṭabaqāt al-ṣūfiya* (Generations of Sufis). Abū Nuʿaym al-Iṣfahānī (d. 1038), another important traditionist and hagiographer, was in turn a student of Sulamī. Abū ʾl-Qāsim al-Qushayrī (d. 1072), author of the most influential text of early Sufism, the *Risāla* (Treatise), following the death of his own master, Abū ʿAlī al-Daqqāq, joined the circle of Sulamī's disciples, which represented the tradition of Iraqi Sufism in Khurasan. ʿAlī ibn ʿUthmān al-Hujwīrī (d. 1070s), author of the first treatise on Sufism written in Persian, the *Kashf al-maḥjūb* (Revealing the Veiled), studied under Abu ʾl-Faḍl al-Khuttalī, through whom he is linked to Shiblī and the Baghdad school. These initiatory and genealogical lines are evidence enough to show the importance of Shiblī for the history of Sufism.

In terms of methodology, I do not seek to present a full-scale biography. The sources ranging from the tenth to the fifteenth centuries, which are relied on here, are not historical documents as such that allow us to gain solid information on Shiblī's life beyond the basics. They were not written for biographical purposes, but rather to preserve anecdotes of his teachings, sayings, and deeds with a purpose in mind, to show his piety as a model for emulation. R. Stephen Humphreys, writing about Louis Massignon's monumental *Passion of al-Ḥallāj*, states that "In terms of hard facts, we have only a skeleton of al-Ḥallāj's career, and much of what we are told about him is saintly hagiography rather than earth-bound history." Massignon's goal, however, was "not to establish a chronology of al-Ḥallāj's actions, but somehow to penetrate to the core of his spiritual personality, and to see it as a vital response to the totality of his milieu."[4] The same applies in many ways to Shiblī and the present investigation, and my hope is to capture the essence of his spirituality, though of course I do not pretend to anything like the depth and scope of Massignon's famous work.

Not every possible source has been consulted, only those representative and better-known works from the tenth to the fifteenth centuries. These writings offer different characterizations, and though there are many gaps, the central personality of Shiblī revealed in these texts usually has a claim to truth. Thus, I hope to present a dynamic and multifaceted portrait of Shiblī, how he was seen by succeeding generations of Sufi and non-Sufi writers from only a few years after his death (Sarrāj) through to the fifteenth century (Jāmī).

Each text is considered separately, its characteristics and qualities, as well as its contribution to our knowledge of Shiblī (in chapters 3 to 13). The value and shortcomings of these works are then considered summarily in chapters 14 and 15. Further aspects of his legacy are discussed in the following chapters, the structure of his sayings (chapter 16), and his relationship with the most famous of his contemporaries, Junayd and Ḥallāj (chapters 17 and 18, respectively). The vexed question of his insanity and how this is perceived particularly by modern scholars is pursued in chapter 19. An analysis of Shiblī's poetry—its style and forms, and examples of his verse—is the subject of chapter 20. Finally, a survey of his Qur'ān exegesis is undertaken in chapter 21, again with many illustrative examples. In this way it is hoped that a rounded picture of Shiblī may emerge by a variety of means, including the anecdotes found in the Sufi manuals and hagiographies, his sayings and poetry preserved in these same works, and his Qur'ān exegesis from Sulamī's early collections.

As mentioned above, my intent is not to produce a comprehensive biography using all the premodern sources. Rather, I seek to offer exemplary and characteristic vignettes from each source, highlighting the differences and the reappraisals of successive generations of Sufi hagiographers. In this way a historically conscious understanding is built up, so we can discern how different generations and communities came to perceive the life and heritage of Shiblī. As for the question of whether we can come to a more informed view of his significance, and perhaps peel away some of the layers of legend and tradition, the following chapters will tell.

CHAPTER 2

The Historical Context

It seems likely that Shiblī was born in Samarra, Iraq, in 861, or perhaps in Baghdad, where he later settled. His birth in Samarra to a family with high political connections is probable given the temporary sojourn of the court and army in that city between 836 and 870. These were years of great disturbance, as the Abbasid caliphate was losing control on power and in rapid decline. The employment of slave soldiers, Transoxanian and Turkish in origin, was an attempt to provide security to the Baghdad regime, but these only inflamed the local populace and former Arab armies. With the removal of military and administrative functions to the new city of Samarra, the central government was further weakened, and, despite much bloodshed, foreign troops failed to provide stability to the tottering regime.[1]

Shiblī's family most likely had their origins in Transoxania, in a village or perhaps small province known as Usrūshana (or Ushrūsana), not far from Samarkand.[2] Shiblī himself seems to have been an official of the Abbasid court in Samarra, perhaps a chamberlain of the caliph's brother Abū Aḥmad al-Muwaffaq. With a privileged and wealthy background, Shiblī received a suitable education, distinguishing himself as a scholar of the Mālikī school of law, and as a student of *ḥadīth*.[3] At about the age of forty he met the Sufi teacher Khayr al-Nassāj of Samarra (d. 934), and embarked on the mystical life. The details are none too precise. The number 40 itself has significant typological associations: the Prophet's experience of revelation at age forty; the commissioning of God's "friends" at age forty; the forty days of spiritual retreat; the forty *ḥadīth* collections; and so on.[4] Moreover, there is some controversy regarding the abruptness of Shiblī's "conversion." Was this due simply to the power of Khayr's persuasion, or due to Shiblī (or a fellow official) being removed suddenly from office, as suggested by some, admittedly late thirteenth-century sources?[5] In any case, if Shiblī was about forty years old when he "converted" to the Sufi path, this would have occurred around the year 900.

Khayr al-Nassāj was renowned as an eloquent preacher (so Hujwīrī), and this may have swayed Shiblī and others, such as Ibrahīm Khawwāṣ (d. 904), to a change of life. Khayr was a student of the influential Sarī Saqaṭī (d. 867), who was Junayd's uncle and mentor. The Persian-writing chronicler and hagiographer, Alī ibn ʿUthmān al-Hujwīrī (d. 1070s), writes that Khayr sent Shiblī on to Junayd (in Baghdad), out of respect for Junayd. He adds that the respect was mutual.[6] This means that Khayr wanted Shiblī to benefit from Junayd's expertise and authority as a Sufi master. Shiblī must then have been his disciple during the last few years of Junayd's life until the latter's death in 910. The intensity of this master-novice relationship became legendary in Sufi lore, and is explored further in chapter 17.

Once Shiblī embarks on his mystical career, there are only a few datable events or details that we can glean. Yet his life coincided with momentous political and social turmoil in the declining years of the Abbasid empire. The devolution of power in the provinces meant the rise of local dynasties, often with the help of slave or foreign armies. The caliphal government could not then rely on tax revenues, and the sale of rights to collect taxes led to widespread corruption in the bureaucracies. Iraq itself saw a prolonged uprising of Zanj slave laborers. The Saffarid dynasty seized control from India through Khurasan and then into western Iran and Iraq. By 905 caliphal authority was restored somewhat, but this proved only a temporary pause in a long decline that ended about the time of Shiblī's death.

During the early 900s, the Shiʿa once again became a major form of popular resistance to Abbasid power. Ismaʿili agitation found expression in the rebellions known as the Qarmaṭian movement, with which Ḥallāj was associated. There were attacks and uprisings in Iraq, Syria, Arabia—the pilgrimage routes and Mecca itself—while the Fatamid dynasty, inspired by Ismaʿili ideas, took control in North Africa and Egypt.

By 935 the empire had devolved into regional autonomy, to the extent that the caliphate ruled only the region around Baghdad. After great struggle and intrigue, the Buwayhid dynasty took control of the city in 945, just before the time of Shiblī's death.[7]

Despite his living through these "interesting times," however, only one important factor seems to have had a discernible impact on Shiblī's thought and behavior. This was the political and religious ramifications associated with the career, and especially the trial and execution in 922, of Shiblī's friend Ḥallāj. The relationship between these two idiosyncratic mystics is explored in chapter 18. Suffice it to say here that Ḥallāj, the political and religious activist, bold and outspoken, was in clear contrast with Shiblī, the political quietist, temperamentally introverted, despite his periods of self-assertion. Shiblī seemed haunted by the specter of Ḥallāj's notoriety and consequent death, and this may have precipitated his refuge into madness.

As we shall see, most of the stories and sayings of Shiblī have little or no connection with contemporary society or politics. They have a purely religious, ethical, or psychological content expected in tales of a Sufi. There are, of course, some exceptions to this. One is the mention of famine in Baghdad, and Shiblī's failure to provide for his own family while he helped others with food. This reflects dire times in the imperial city, but such anecdotes center on Shiblī and the ethics of his actions, not on the actual historical circumstances.

A further intimation found in the source writings concerns his wealth and privilege, and the probability of continued political connections throughout his life. There is a suggestion that his material wealth may have embarrassed him, given his ascetic temper. This would account for some of the emblematic stories about his extravagance, throwing away money or burning expensive clothes, perfumes, and the like. There is also the mention of his having servants to attend him, for example later in life, and in the narratives about his death. Yet as a Sufi teacher he would naturally have a circle of students who would see to his daily needs.

Among others, his most important students were Abu ʾl-Qāsim al-Naṣrābādhī (d. 977–978) and Abu ʾl-Ḥasan al-Ḥuṣrī (d. 982). Naṣrābādhī was initiated as a Sufi by Shiblī in 942, and is recognised as a link between the latter and Abū ʿAbd al-Raḥmān al-Sulamī (d. 1021), the foremost traditionist and biographer of the early Sufi movement. Naṣrābādhī resided for some time in Nishapur, Sulamī's hometown, and apparently made the pilgrimage with him. Another Nishapurian and important chronicler of early Sufism, Abu ʾl-Qāsim al-Qushayrī (d. 1072), is also related to Naṣrābādhī through Qushayrī's master, Abū ʿAlī al-Daqqāq (d. 1015), who was his student. These two prominent Sufi authors thus have a direct link to Shiblī's teachings through Naṣrābādhī.

As mentioned in the Introduction, the Persian-writing author, ʿAlī ibn ʿUthmān al-Hujwīrī, is linked to Shiblī and Junayd through Shiblī's disciple Abu ʾl-Ḥasan al-Ḥuṣrī, who taught Hujwīrī's master, Abu ʾl-Faḍl al-Khuttalī (d. ?). In this way, Persian Sufi writers preserved the Baghdad traditions directly. The famous Persian traditionist and hagiographer, ʿAbdallāh Anṣārī of Herat (d. 1089), wrote that Ḥuṣrī was Shiblī's only disciple in the sense that others "heard his words," but only Ḥuṣrī was his "inheritor." Conversely, Ḥuṣrī had no other master than Shiblī, and was deeply versed in his teaching. Anṣārī also reports that Shiblī once said to his student: "You are insane as I am; between us there is an eternal affection and harmony!"[8]

Again there are few details concerning Shiblī's family, since it was customary not to mention wife/wives and children, even in biographical writings. There are some indications, however—for example, the mention of shaving his beard, and his wife cutting her hair, on the death of one of their sons.[9] The ascetic practice of withdrawal from family was apparently not followed; this was more part of Christian and Indian traditions than it ever was in Islam, as many famous Sufis, including Junayd, lived with their families.

By the time of Shiblī's death in 946, the Abbasids' grip on power had come to an end, though the caliphate continued nominally for another three centuries. During these years Sufi theory came to be systematized, and the stories and sayings of the Sufi pioneers were collected and recorded. It is in these writings that Shiblī's heritage has come down to us, and we must turn to these to further our investigation of his life and thought.

SHIBLĪ IN THE SOURCES

Chapter 3

Sarrāj's *Book of Illuminations*

The earliest existing source for the life and sayings of Shiblī is the tenth-century treatise on Sufism, the *Kitāb al-lumaʿ fi ʾl-taṣawwuf* (Book of Illuminations About the Sufi Path) of Abū Naṣr al-Sarrāj (d. 988). This foundational text is a comprehensive systematization of Sufi theory and practice that has a clear apologetic purpose, to demonstrate the conformity of Sufi principles with the Qurʾān and the *sunna* or Path of the Prophet.

The author, Abū Naṣr al-Sarrāj from Ṭūs in Khurasan (northeast Iran), has handed down a rich source of early Muslim piety, a mine of valuable documentary information on the formative centuries of Sufism. We do not have much detail about Sarrāj's life, apart from his association with the city of Ṭūs, and his reputation as a Sunni ascetic and scholar. It is known that he traveled widely to collect authentic materials for his scholarly activity and writings. He died in Ṭūs in 988, having finished his major work, the *Lumaʿ*, which shows the judgments of a mature and independent mind.

Sarrāj details the thought and teaching of Islamic mysticism, its technical vocabulary, the stages of the spiritual path, as well as the manners and customs of the Sufi pioneers. In a typical chapter of the *Lumaʿ* we might find a topic discussed first from the perspective of the Qurʾān, second from that of *ḥadīth,* and third from the reported sayings or incidents in the lives of the Sufi masters that illustrate their approach, theoretical or practical, to the issue in question. Thus, we have documented for us a whole variety of important information that is a valuable source for our knowledge and understanding of people such as Shiblī.

Alexander Knysh associates Sarrāj with the early Sufi historian Jaʿfar al-Khuldī (d. 959–960) and thus with Junayd's circle in Baghdad. He was also friendly with a leading representative of Junayd in southern Iran, Ibn Khafīf al-Shīrāzī (d. 982). Sarrāj also had contact with al-Tustarī's disciples in Basra, the Sālimīya school, including their leader, Aḥmad b. Sālim (d. 967).[1] Knysh argues that these affiliations exposed Sarrāj to a variety of regional and doctrinal trends in the early mystical movement. In spite of his Khurasanian background, however, he is an exponent of Iraqi Sufism.

According to this view, the *Luma*ʿ is a full critical analysis of doctrines and practices, Sarrāj wishing to demonstrate Sufism's roots in the earliest Islamic traditions. He tries to trace its origins back to the time of the Prophet and his companions, these being the paragons of piety worthy of emulation. Moreover, the Sufis are on a par with the *ḥadīth* experts and scholar-jurists, indeed they are preeminent over them, being the only ones who live up to the piety of the first Muslims.[2]

Sarrāj elucidates ideas, practices, and terminology, devoting chapters to discussions of states and stages of the mystical path, miracles, controversial utterances and rules of companionship. He also addresses theoretical and practical errors made by some. He does not conceal his own views, showing himself to be a "sober" and scholarly Sufi in the pattern of Junayd. Yet he is open minded and generous in his detailing and defence of the ecstatic utterances of Abū Yazīd al-Basṭāmī (d. 875), and indeed of Shiblī, dedicating several chapters to both these men.[3]

Ahmet Karamustafa, on the other hand, argues that the *Luma*ʿ was not a blending of native, Khurasanian traditions with the spreading Iraqi version, but rather a simple importation of the latter. Sarrāj purportedly wrote the *Luma*ʿ because of the diffusion of false and spurious accounts of Sufism, and the need to set forth the truth about this misunderstood phenomenon. In this he succeeded spectacularly.[4]

Karamustafa, like Knysh, also notes that Sarrāj neither shied away from addressing controversial and disputed subjects, nor from offering his own opinions. His candid discussion and detailing of those Sufis who had clearly fallen into error and apostasy is a sign of his confidence in the secure Islamic foundations of the mystical movement. Thus Karamustafa sees the *Luma*ʿ as a presentation of Iraqi-based Sufism, minus its doubtful excesses, to a Khurasanian readership largely unfamiliar with this recent phenomenon. Sarrāj, in this view, was probably not a Sufi master himself but rather a scholar, and his astute survey has made him one of the earliest genuine observers of Sufi history.[5]

Despite the great advantage we have from Sarrāj's documentation, it is important to remember that much of this valuable material is secondary to the author's main purpose, and comes to us only incidentally as part of his work. In using the *Lumaʿ* as a source for the biography and teaching of Shiblī, we should bear in mind that such documentation is not the intended purpose of the book, and our exploiting this resource is somewhat fortuitous. For example, a particular incident relating to Shiblī may not have the importance in his life story implied by its inclusion in the *Lumaʿ*. What appears in Sarrāj's work is probably rather more circumstantial than what a devoted biography might include. Thus, the picture we build of Shiblī is a somewhat haphazard portrait. It depends on details recorded for theological reasons, for purposes of teaching, moral instruction, guidance and emulation, not for biographical reasons.

As for the historical value of the anecdotes and sayings in Sarrāj's work, their authenticity and reliability, some general remarks apply as they do to the many other early Sufi works considered in the present book. First, there is no question that there are many historically doubtful and fabricated anecdotes relating to early Sufi figures, such as Shiblī, which have found their way into these writings. Examples of paradigmatic narratives abound, that is, much the same events related to two or more different Sufi figures. Such repetitions and variants should urge caution on our use of these narratives as hard biographical data. It is important to remember that from a very early stage, the anecdotes that circulated about different Sufi masters were designed to promote their piety and worthiness of emulation, rather than disclose what actually happened to them during their lifetime.

We may presume that Sarrāj, writing only a generation or so after Shiblī's death, would have ascertained the facts before committing these narratives to the page. This presumption generally cannot be upheld, however, for often the greatest fabrication of anecdotes is carried out by family or followers soon after the event, soon after the death of the esteemed person in order to promote their claim to sanctity. What is also apparent is that there was probably a large "reservoir" of anecdotes available to compilers and editors, since different stories and sayings appear for the first time in compilations made many centuries after the earliest works. Thus, later writings do not simply recycle earlier ones, as will become clear in the later chapters of the present book.

In brief, therefore, we cannot be sure of the authenticity of many of the anecdotes and sayings we find in this early work by Sarrāj. On the other hand, the "authentic character" of Shiblī, the outlines of his temperament and piety, often ring true in many narratives, just as we have the "authentic character" of Junayd in his "sobriety," cautiousness, and probity. The historical positivist will be rather disappointed by the lack of "objective" reliability of these sources, but we do have the portrait of these early Sufi figures such as Shiblī painted in the way that their near-contemporaries wished them to be seen and remembered.

In drawing on the *Kitāb al-luma*ʿ as a source for the life and sayings of Shiblī, I have collated the material thematically, given the size and range of the data available.

THE NATURE OF KNOWLEDGE

By the time of Shiblī's maturity in the early years of the tenth century, concepts of knowledge had already developed to a high level of sophistication in the Sufi tradition. Though in the Qurʾān the usual term for knowledge of various types was *ʿilm,* this word soon became restricted to rational, intellectual, or learned knowledge, while the Sufis came to use *maʿrifa* for more intimate, experiential, mystical ways of knowing. Further refinements involved the term *dhawq,* the immediate experience of "tasting" or direct perception of the Real. This mode of awareness overrides all other types of knowledge. Shiblī was once asked about the state of the knower (*ʿārif*) when he comes to "see" (*bi-mashhad*) the Real (*al-ḥaqq*). He answered by saying that when this seer begins to perceive, the senses and physical perceptions disappear and die away. Shiblī was also asked what was the beginning and end of this appraisal. He says its beginning is knowledge (*maʿrifa*) of it, and its end is becoming one with it.[6] By this Shiblī probably means that as physical perceptions fade, the subject becomes identified with the "object" of perception, so that subject-object becomes a false dichotomy, as experienced in intense meditation. In modern psychological terms, the "intentional trinities of subject-perceiving-object and the subject-thinking-thought are abolished. Rather than a knowledge-by-acquaintance, one is instructed to let go of intentional knowledge altogether, and come to rest 'in' or 'through' one's awareness alone."[7] Shiblī continues, in this same passage, stating that the sign of knowledge is to see oneself in the "grip of Majesty" (*ʿizza*) and to let the vicissitudes of fate pass by. He also says that the sign of knowledge is love, since one who knows Him loves Him.[8]

In another section of the *Lumaʿ*, Shiblī is reported to have said that there are three "tongues" or languages, which can be understood as three ways of knowing. The first is the tongue of acquired knowledge (*ʿilm*), which comes to us via intermediaries such as the senses. The second is the tongue of Reality (*al-ḥaqīqa*), which God conveys to the inmost heart (*al-asrār*) without intermediaries. The third is the tongue of the Truth or the Real (*al-ḥaqq*), which has no path to it. By this Shiblī probably means either that it is ineffable, or that its action is wholly mysterious.[9]

In another context, Shiblī is reported as saying that for every sign with which people point to the Truth or the Real (*al-ḥaqq*) there is reciprocity, since they point to the Truth by the Truth; to this there is no other way.[10]

THE EXPERIENCE OF UNITY OR ONENESS (TAWḤĪD)

On being questioned about the nature of *tawḥīd* (experience of unity or oneness), Shiblī speaks only of its ineffability and the folly of attempting to describe it, though elsewhere he does occasionally attempt this. Such ineffability, explained in modern terms, "supports the thought that certain mystical experiences are beyond language and expectations, and indeed are outside the usual necessary relationships between language and experience."[11] In Sarrāj's chapter on *tawḥīd*, Shiblī answers a questioner who asks about its nature: "Woe to you! One who replies to a question on *tawḥīd* by means of an explanation is an apostate (*mulḥid*); and one who alludes or gives a sign to it is a dualist . . . ; one who imagines that he has arrived [at *tawḥīd*] has achieved nothing; and one who points toward it is an idol worshipper," and so on.[12] Sarrāj comments on this lengthy saying of Shiblī's by saying that what he intended was to point out the utter distinction of the eternal from the created, and that people are only able to describe or refer to what appears to them in their experience.

In another context Shiblī is reported to have said that one who apprehends the least mote of knowledge about *tawḥīd* becomes too weak to bear the weight of a bug or beetle (*baqqa*) because of the heaviness of the burden of knowledge! He is also quoted as saying that one who comprehends a mote of knowledge about *tawḥīd* bears the heavens and the earth on a hair of their eyelid.[13]

Despite Shiblī's strictures on the folly of trying to explain *tawḥīd,* he is reported as saying that God makes you experience unity and sets you apart for Himself, and makes you see this, though He hides your seeing from you.[14] In modern psychological terms, "Removing both conceptual knowledge, knowledge-about, and sensory contact, knowledge-by-acquaintance, . . . one comes to employ knowledge-by-identity alone. 'That' which one knows when knowing one is aware is *all* that is recalled after he or she has continued 'void of conceptions.' "[15]

ASCETICISM: SAYINGS AND DEEDS

The ascetic attitude is not just withdrawal from and renunciation of the world, but more radically, withdrawal and renunciation of the physical senses.[16] This is the reasoning behind the Sufis' objective of God-consciousness, of not neglecting to have God in mind for a single moment. The following points are merely illustrative of Shiblī's approach to asceticism.

Asked to define piety (*waraʿ*), Shiblī says that it is to be heedful or cautious (*tatawarraʿa*) that your heart is not distracted from God for the twinkling of an eye.[17] This sentiment and variants of it recur often in the anecdotes relating to Shiblī.

Sarrāj notes that the Sufi adepts "renounce and repent of their renunciation." Thus Shiblī, being asked about renunciation (*zuhd*) said: 'Renunciation is neglect, because the world is nothing and renunciation of nothing is neglect."[18]

In a similar vein, Shiblī has such scant regard for the physical world that he expresses his disdain in the following related sayings. He said that if the world was but a morsel of food in a child's mouth he would feel pity for the child. This is presumably because of the morsel's insubstantiality. Pseudo-ʿAṭṭār, the unknown author of Shiblī's biography appended to the genuine Farīd al-Dīn ʿAṭṭār's *Tadhkirat al-awliyā*ʾ (Memorial of God's Friends), repeats this saying but adds, "because the child would go hungry."[19] Sarrāj goes on to report Shiblī's saying that if the world was a morsel he would eat it and so leave humankind no intermediary with God.[20]

As an example of ascetic practice, Shiblī mentions that when he began the Sufi path he would smear his eyes with salt to ward off sleep. If the temptation of sleep increased he would also heat collyrium and rub this into his eyes.[21] This statement provides an insight into Shiblī's way of life, and illustrates the type of austerity he underwent. In fact, this is one of the characteristic elements of his asceticism mentioned by Ibn Khallikān in the biographical entry on Shiblī in his famous dictionary.[22] Always ready to elaborate, pseudo-ʿAṭṭār adds that he is said to have used seven maunds of salt in this way (a maund being a variable but substantial weight, depending on region and date).[23]

PATIENCE AND DEPENDENCE ON GOD

An important anecdote from Shiblī's life, which deals with "patience" (*ṣabr*) is illustrative of the quality of long-suffering or endurance, which is included in the semantic range of the Arabic term. Mention has already been made in chapter 1 of the story about when Shiblī was a patient in the Baghdad hospital, and some of his friends came to visit. Perhaps feigning ignorance, he asked who they were; the friends answered that they were the people who loved him. He began to throw stones at them and they ran away. He called after them: "Liars! You claim to be my friends, but you cannot endure my testing!"[24] The context of this incident is of interest, as it provides one of the few clues in early sources that he spent time in the Baghdad hospital, evidently suffering from mental illness, Sarrāj noting that he was shackled with chains. There are very few other early references to his illness, but by the eleventh century and later a tradition had developed of narratives concerning his mental derangement. In fact pseudo-ʿAṭṭār had such a wealth of anecdotes that he was able to contextualize this incident within a structure relating to the course of his hospitalization. Sarrāj, on the other hand, has left only this single anecdote, which is a tantalizing fragment of a larger picture.

Shiblī was asked by an unnamed questioner about the most difficult aspect of patience. Shiblī suggested three possible responses: patience in God, patience for God, and patience with God. When the questioner refused to accept any of these responses, Shiblī grew angry and demanded a reply. The man responded: patience without God, whereupon Shiblī let out a great cry. He realized the cogency of the man's answer, that patience in the absence of God's reassuring presence is a most difficult circumstance for the believer.[25]

The attitude of dependence and trust in God (*tawakkul*) features often in Sufi life. Complete dependence on God, often without any intermediaries such as reliance on other people or on everyday sustenance, is frequently portrayed as a practical assertion of strong faith. Asked about *tawakkul*, Shiblī answered succinctly and profoundly: "That you should belong to God as if you did not exist and that God Most High should belong to you as if He never ceased to exist."[26]

ECSTASY AND MYSTICAL EXPERIENCE

That Shiblī was an "intoxicated" mystic, one who placed high value on ecstatic experience, was acknowledged by his contemporaries, and is not a retrospective label. Thus, Junayd is reported to have said that Shiblī was "intoxicated" and that if he were to recover from this he would be an excellent leader.[27] Junayd's characteristic "sobriety" leads him to rue Shiblī's "drunkenness" and to wish for his transformation.

Shiblī's emotional receptivity led him to experience sudden changes of state, of ecstasy or bewilderment, depending on the circumstances. On one occasion, when made psychologically responsive by fasting in the month of Ramadan, he is reported to have cried out, turned pale and began trembling on hearing a Qur'ānic verse being recited in a mosque.[28] On this occasion the verse was one of threat: "If We pleased, We could take away what We have revealed to you . . ." (Qur'ān 17:86). Shiblī's response was to repeat over and over in a type of involuntary state: "Thus do lovers converse!" In this, he is casting himself in the role of the scorned lover of God, hearing the divine threat as lovers' converse. (See further chapter 7 on Qushayrī's *Risāla* for an extended interpretation of this anecdote.)

Shiblī would go into ecstasies (e.g., *yatawājada*) frequently on hearing secular or popular poetry being recited, as well as the Qur'ān, as Sarrāj reports.[29] He would also frequently utter ecstatic sayings in this state, such as on one occasion when he went into ecstasies and said: "Oh, no-one except Him knows what is in my heart!"[30]

Shiblī would also experience states of bewilderment that found him expressing ecstatic utterances. Someone saw him in an anxious state, and asked why this was: "Is not He with you, and you with Him?" Shiblī replied: "Were I to be with Him, then I would be myself, but I am effaced in what He is,"[31] upon which Sarrāj comments: "nothing is from me, nor in me, nor apart from me, but all is from Him, in Him and to Him."[32]

Shiblī spoke of two types of bewilderment (*ḥayra*), one from excessive fear of committing evil, and the other from the revelation of (God's) majesty to hearts.[33] Such an utterance loses its great force in being translated or paraphrased into a language other than Arabic, since the original is a finely crafted set of balanced phrases in rhymed prose (*saj*ʿ), a not infrequent feature of his sayings.

Sarrāj also records part of a letter written by Shiblī to Junayd, in which he describes a bewildering mystical state akin to madness, as Shiblī acknowledges. He stresses the overwhelming and enduring nature of the state, how it effaces any vision of the divine, makes the imagination withdraw, makes tongues dumb, and blots out acquired knowledge. The upshot is that it overwhelms the reason, requiring the sufferer to be bound with shackles. Sarrāj also records Junayd's reply in which he reprimands Shiblī for divulging in public what other Sufis kept secret, a characteristic criticism of Junayd's.[34]

Sarrāj presents a short discourse on Shiblī's experience of *waqt*, the instantaneous "moment" of mystical insight. Shiblī claims rather boastfully to his hearers that "your 'moments' are disjointed, whereas mine do not have any limits," that is, these states are longer lasting or more pervasive.[35] Sarrāj adds that here Shiblī may have been speaking an ecstatic utterance (*shaṭḥ*), as with the following statement in which he says cryptically: "I am my momentary state, and it is precious to me; there is only I in this state, and I am effaced." This self-referential description of a mystical state is again characterized as knowledge-by-identity, in the words of Robert Forman: "Although this encounter is beyond words, in it one has a direct and permanent experience of the self-referential nature of consciousness itself."[36]

Sarrāj offers an extended explanation of these ecstatic sayings, though his explanation is sometimes as cryptic as Shiblī's original statements. At one point, however, Sarrāj gives a sort of "definition" of *waqt*: he says that the term "alludes to the moment [*nafas*] which is between the two breaths [*nafasayn*], and the thought [*khāṭir*] which is between two thoughts [*khāṭirayn*]; if these are in God and to God, this is *waqt*."[37]

QURʾĀNIC EXPLANATIONS

Sarrāj records a substantial amount of Qurʾānic exegesis attributed to the early Sufi masters, devoting several chapters of the *Lumaʿ* to this topic. The importance of early Sufi *tafsīr* has been highlighted by the researches of scholars such as Paul Nwyia and Gerhard Böwering. It is clear that devotions and meditations on the Qurʾān allowed the Sufis a unique insight into its meaning, symbolism, and mystical import. Shiblī's singular worldview led him to express some novel interpretations of the Muslim scriptures, which form an integral part of his sayings. A later chapter of the present book is devoted to his exegesis taken from the definitive collections of Abū ʿAbd al-Raḥmān al-Sulamī (d. 1021), but the following examples are those contained in Sarrāj's *Lumaʿ*.

Some examples are recorded that illustrate the method of semantic hermeneutic (*fahm*) rather than symbolic or allusive exegesis (*ishāra;* this distinction is Sarrāj's: *Lumaʿ* pp. 90ff). Shiblī is asked to comment on the first part of verse Qurʾān 24:30: "tell believing men to lower their gaze. . . ." He offers a dual interpretation of this partial verse, an esoteric (*bāṭin*) and exoteric (*ẓāhir*) explanation, which makes sense only if this part-verse is cited in isolation from its context. Shiblī comments that one should lower the gaze of the eyes from what is forbidden (the *ẓāhir* sense), and the gaze of hearts from anything other than God (the *bāṭin* sense).[38] Unfortunately the context nullifies the force of the esoteric interpretation, as the verse continues to speak unambiguously in terms of the exoteric (referring to bodily modesty and chastity).

Nevertheless, this illustrates the dextrous use of rather mundane verses of the Qurʾān to yield anagogical interpretations. It should be noted that the authorship of this explanation is disputed, since Sulamī in his *Ḥaqāʾiq al-tafsīr* cites Abū ʾl-ʿAbbās Ibn ʿAṭāʾ (d. 922) as the author of this comment.[39]

Shiblī is also questioned about the meaning of Qurʾān 50:37: "There truly is in this a reminder for whoever has a heart, whoever listens attentively." The *crux* here is the expression "whoever has a heart," which traditional commentators (*Tafsīr al-Jalālayn* and Bayḍāwī to some extent) explain as "reason" or "understanding." Shiblī, however, has a rather different interpretation, commenting "to one whose heart is [toward] God."[40] He immediately explains his meaning by citing a couplet of poetry:

> I have not a weary heart toward you;
> all my limbs are hearts toward you.

Shiblī was once asked about the interpretation of the contentious verse Qurʾān 3:54: "The [disbelievers] schemed but God also schemed; God is the Best of Schemers." The questioner understood the situation of the disbelievers' scheming, but what was the occasion of God's scheming? Shiblī answered that God left them to their own devices in their scheming, and if He had willed to change their hearts He would have done so.[41] Shiblī immediately sensed that the questioner was not satisfied with his response, so he recited an apposite couplet of verse:

> 'For me the deed is ugly coming from someone other than you,
> then when you do this, it is beautiful coming from you!'

This verse seeks to explain the difficulty of God's scheming or plotting (*makr*) mentioned in the Qurʾānic verse. That this verse was a problem is also attested to in Sulamī's *Ḥaqāʾiq al-tafsīr*, where a similar question is posed as to how scheming can be attributed to God. The unnamed respondent suggested that there is no (knowable) cause for His actions, and the same couplet of verse is quoted.[42] However, Shiblī here seems to be engaging with the arguments of *kalām*, specifically the Muʿtazilites, for whom an evil or sinful deed had to be seen as *intrinsically* evil. By suggesting that the act becomes "beautiful" when considered from the point of view of its divine origin, he challenges the Muʿtazilite conception of evil or sinful acts.

ECCENTRIC BEHAVIOR

Toward the end of the *Kitāb al-lumaʿ*, Sarrāj devotes several chapters to explaining the unusual or controversial sayings and deeds of various Sufis, including Shiblī and Abū Yazīd al-Basṭāmī. In one of these apologetic chapters Sarrāj discusses the issue of Shiblī's apparent extravagance, for instance, reports that he burned precious clothes and foods, and his being criticized for selling valuable real estate without giving any of the proceeds to his needy family.[43] Sarrāj offers several apologies for these seemingly wasteful actions. First he suggests that money not spent sinfully is not wasted. Next he cites some lengthy *ḥadīths*, for example, one about Abū Bakr who gave to the people without providing for his own family; when questioned by the Prophet about what he left for his family, he said that he left them God and His Prophet. Sarrāj also argues that Shiblī burned these precious things to rid his heart of material distractions, claiming that for mystics every distraction from God is their enemy from which they seek freedom.[44]

In a chapter concerning what the Sufis did when they received gifts, Sarrāj relates that once, during a time of drought and starvation, Shiblī was given a large sum of money, which he proceeded to give away to every poor person, leaving none for his own hungry family. This is evidently a variant on the anecdote about the real estate proceeds mentioned above. His friend Abū ʿAbdallāh al-Ḥuṣrī (d. ?; not Shiblī's disciple of the same surname) had to buy food for them.[45] This is another, perhaps paradigmatic, story illustrating Shiblī's generosity and his disregard for the fortunes of his own family.

EXTRAORDINARY SAYINGS

In a chapter discussing the unusual sayings and expressions used by the Sufis, Sarrāj records Shiblī's explanation of the phrase "I am you and you are I." This poetic expression recalls the Majnūn-

Laylā tradition in Arabic legend, and Shiblī refers to this tradition in his discussion. He recalls that Majnūn the insane lover would say "I am Laylā" when asked about her, having melded his identity with his beloved: "he would hide himself in Laylā from Laylā, . . . [and] from every notion other than Laylā, and he perceived all things through Laylā."[46] Shiblī also illustrates this expression of identity with an anecdote about two lovers who were traveling by sea; one of them fell from the ship and was about to drown when the other threw himself into the water. After both were rescued by a diver, the first lover asked the second why he had thrown himself into the sea, to which he replied "I am hidden in you from myself; I thought that I was you."[47] The metaphor of the sea in Sufi parlance, the "sea" of the soul or the "sea" of Unity or God's bounty, would not be lost on Shiblī's listeners.

This melding of identity is further explored in a chapter devoted to Shiblī's extraordinary sayings, where it is recorded that he bade farewell to some friends as if he were God speaking: "Go! I am with you; wherever you may be you are in my care and protection!"[48] Sarrāj explains this identity fusion as a result of his overpowering mystical state in which his own ego is annihilated (*maḥqan*) in the denuding of the experience of unification (*tajrīd al-tawḥīd*): "When he says 'I' he is giving expression to his altered state [*wajd*] and translating his mystical state [*ḥāl*] which has taken possession of his inmost heart."[49]

A perplexing action is of Shiblī taking a piece of bread from an unnamed person and eating it, saying: "My base soul [*nafs*] sought a piece of bread from me, and had I turned my inmost heart [*sir*] toward the heavenly Throne and Chair, it would certainly have been burned up!"[50] Sarrāj comments that he found in his inmost heart a trace of Unity and the Preeternal, whereas the Throne and Chair are created entities brought into being by divine fiat. Perhaps the meaning here is that for his heart, having a trace of the Eternal, to turn toward the created Throne as other-than-God would be an act of polytheism (*shirk*), and thus deserving the condemnation of hellfire.

In another chapter dealing with Shiblī's sayings, it is recorded that he said: "I move toward the infinite, but I see only the finite; and I move to the right and to the left toward the infinite, but I see only the finite; then I return and see all of this in a hair of my little finger!"[51] Sarrāj offers an explanation, unfortunately marred by textual lacunae, but again referring to the Throne and Chair as created entities, and to God's singular knowledge of the infinite not available to humankind.[52] The reference to the hair of his little finger is understood as the microcosm containing all the immensity of the created world within the smallest and most insignificant compass.

The theme of turning his heart toward the Throne is continued in another utterance in which he implores: "O God, if You know of any residue of other-than-You in me, then burn me up with Your fire—there is no god but You!"[53] These are the words of a fervent unitarian, assiduously aware of the possibility of having regard for anything other than God, which constitutes in his overscrupulous eyes the heinous sin of polytheism. Sarrāj comments that such statements emanate from an altered mystical state, which is a transitory event. Its transitoriness is a grace from God, for if it were permanent it would render null and void all religious, moral, and social laws and responsibilities.[54]

The theme of hellfire continues with Shiblī reported as saying: "If I thought that hell with its fires and flames would burn a single hair of mine, I would be a polytheist!"[55] Sarrāj guides us to the best interpretation of this by commenting that hellfires burn only by God's command; Shiblī implies that attributing independent power to hell is an act of polytheism, of regarding as important something other-than-God. Shiblī continues on this theme, questioning the value of hellfire, claiming that coming face to face with God while estranged from Him is a much harsher punishment than hell.

SHIBLĪ'S DEATH

Two accounts of Shiblī's death are recorded in the *Luma*ʿ. Both have a common motif, namely that his servant, Bundār (or Bakrān) al-Dīnawarī, forgot to run water through Shiblī's beard while washing him in preparation for prayer.[56] This lapse was made good by the moribund Shiblī grabbing his servant's hand and guiding him to perform the correct ritual. This was apparently the most remarkable aspect of Shiblī's last hours, and we are given no information on the illness or other circumstances accompanying his death.

Both these accounts serve a similar purpose, namely to show the exemplary piety of Shiblī even on his deathbed, that his scrupulous adherence to prescribed rituals did not slacken despite his frailty and nearness to life's end. The second account has Shiblī also mentioning a wrongly obtained *dirhem*, which he begged for in the street, and how this weighed terribly on his mind.[57] A further mention in the *Lumaʿ* of Shiblī's last hours has him reciting the following verse couplets all night:

> 'In every house where you dwell
> there is no need for lamps;
> Your hoped-for countenance is our proof
> on the day when people come with proofs.'[58]

At the end of a series of chapters dealing with Shiblī's unconventional sayings, Sarrāj concludes his discussion by stating "there is much that is related of Shiblī, and it is not possible to mention it all for fear of being long-winded; but the wise person will infer from the small amount given to the greater part not mentioned, and success is with God!"[59] This nicely sums up our own selection of Shiblī's anecdotes and sayings from the *Kitāb al-lumaʿ*; including every reference would be tedious, but we have attempted a representative survey of the available material, aiming to throw light on this remarkable spiritual man.

CHAPTER 4

Kalābādhī's *Book of Understanding*

A near contemporary of Sarrāj, Abū Bakr al-Kalābādhī (d. 990s) was evidently a native of Bukhara, but little else is known about this author. His most famous work, *Kitāb al-taʿarruf li-madhhab ahl al-taṣawwuf* (Book of Understanding Sufi Teachings), is a concise abstract of the main ideas of Sufism, written in an apologetic style, like Sarrāj's work, seeking to explain the mainstream nature of these ideas. The concise yet comprehensive style of Kalābādhī made his book attractive for a wide audience, and it has become one of the foundational reference works of Sufism.

His book consists largely of thematically arranged quotations attributed to the authoritative figures of Iraqi-based Sufism. However, as Alexander Knysh notes, Kalābādhī lived in Bukhara at some distance from the traditional Sufi centers of Iraq and Khurasan. It is thus surprising that the author champions the Baghdad tradition, and Ḥallāj especially, given the latter's controversial career, and conversely he seems to discount the local or even Khurasanian modes of asceticism and mysticism. This indicates the wide diffusion of the Iraqi tradition, even to the far eastern fringes of the former Muslim empire.[1]

Like Sarrāj, Kalābādhī addresses disagreements on matters of theory and practice, and is somewhat reticent in divulging arcane ideas to beginners or outsiders. Perhaps this is due, as Knysh suggests, to the persecution and general upset in the wake of Ḥallāj's martyrdom. In any case, his partiality for Iraqi-style Sufism and lack of regard for native Transoxanian traditions is most remarkable.[2]

Ahmet Karamustafa focuses on the rather "academic" approach of Kalābādhī to his subject, by his not mentioning contemporary Sufi authorities, his own teachers, or written sources. It seems that he learned Sufism in a rather bookish way, from written works, evidently of the Iraqi school, as mentioned above. Karamustafa argues that the work was in fact an introduction to a new subject for Eastern readers. Rather than primarily defending the subject apologetically from detractors or opponents in the wake of Ḥallāj, he is introducing this aspect of mainstream piety to interested but uninformed or misinformed readers and aspirants to the Sufi path.[3]

Because of the brevity of the *Taʿarruf*, Shiblī is not mentioned as frequently as in Sarrāj's *Lumaʿ*, and although there is some overlapping or repetition of material, most of the references are original and appear in Kalābādhī's book for the first time.

The author mentions Shiblī, along with other famous Sufis, as having "published" or distributed (*nashara*) books and letters about the "science of allusions" (*ʿulūm al-ishāra*), that is, discourses on mystical lore and the interpretation of Sufi ideas and sayings.[4] If this statement is correct, it seems that Shiblī's writings have been lost to us, apart from those portions incorporated into other books. This also ties in with the eleventh-century author ʿAlī ibn ʿUthmān al-Hujwīrī's mention of the anecdotes (*ḥikāyāt*) concerning Shiblī, though these may be the extant narratives we possess in the various early sources. In any case it seems that collections of anecdotes or sayings were available to authors in the tenth century and later, which are now lost to us.

Shiblī's scant regard for the world and the worthlessness of renunciation was referred to in the *Kitāb al-lumaʿ* above. In the same vein, Kalābādhī records that when he was questioned about renunciation (*zuhd*), he answered in characteristic fashion: "What value is there in something worth less than a gnat's wing that renunciation needs to be exercised with regard to it?"[5]

In a chapter concerning the meaning of intimacy (*uns*), Shiblī is reported as saying that "it is your estrangement [*waḥsha*] from oneself [*min-hu*]."[6] This terse statement is ambiguous in the extreme. Estrangement seems on the face of it the opposite of intimacy, though in the Sufis' paradoxical language this may well be the meaning. That the reference of *min-hu* is to one's self or one's heart, however, is confirmed by a later statement of Shiblī's in the chapter on unitary experience (*tawḥīd*). There he states: "the servant [of God] does not attain true union until one is estranged from one's inmost heart because of the Real's disclosure to one."[7] This feeling of estrangement is analogous to the modern experience described by Robert Forman: "the feeling inside of being me was like being entirely empty, a perfect vacuum. . . ."[8]

Kalābādhī also records a version of Junayd's characteristic reprimand of Shiblī for disclosing publicly what the Sufis earnestly investigate but conceal "in cellars," that is, their secret teachings.[9] Sarrāj's mention of this reprimand was noted in the previous chapter, but Kalābādhī adds Shiblī's response to Junayd: "I speak and I hear, and is there any other in the two worlds apart from me?" Interestingly, pseudo-ʿAṭṭār in the *Tadhkirat al-awliyāʾ* expands still further on this encounter, adding to the response: "nay there is indeed a word which goes from Real to Real, and Shiblī is not in the middle."[10] Pseudo-ʿAṭṭār is perhaps suggesting that Shiblī is a disinterested conduit of a divine message, that he is only an impartial medium, though it is open to question whether this really explains the original saying.

CHAPTER 5

Sulamī's *Generations of the Sufis*

A Sufi hagiographer and Qur'ān commentator from Nishapur, Abū ʿAbd al-Raḥmān al-Sulamī lived a generation or so later than Sarrāj and Kalābādhī. He was born in about 937 or 942 into a religiously inclined family, his education being entrusted to his maternal grandfather who was a Shāfiʿī scholar and ascetic. Sulamī became an important *ḥadīth* scholar, and traveled widely in pursuit of knowledge. He received an *ijāza* (teaching certificate) from Abū Sahl al-Ṣuʿlūkī (d. 980), and becoming interested in Sufism, gained a Sufi cloak (*khirqa*) from Abu 'l-Qāsim al-Naṣrābādhī, who had been a pupil of Shiblī in Baghdad. Shortly after completing the pilgrimage to the Ḥijāz in 976 with Naṣrābādhī, the latter died, and on returning to Nishapur, Sulamī's teacher Ismāʿīl b. Nujayd had died also, bequeathing him his extensive library. This became the center of a small lodge where Sulamī remained studying and teaching until the end of his life in 1021.[1]

Apart from his Qur'ān commentaries, Sulamī is best known for his extensive biographical work, the *Ṭabaqāt al-ṣūfīya* (Generations of the Sufis), itself a smaller version of a now lost *Ta'rīkh al-ṣūfīya* (Chronology of the Sufis). The extant work has summary biographies of 105 Sufis grouped in roughly chronological sections called *ṭabaqāt* (layers or generations), with short selections of their sayings. In keeping with Sulamī's interest in *ḥadīth,* most of the sayings are introduced with full *isnād* (chain of transmitters), lending a more authoritative "traditionist" character to the work. Sulamī's *Ṭabaqāt* is the earliest dedicated Sufi biographical collection, and the prototype of its genre. It was immensely influential, and the model for numerous later works in both Arabic and Persian, its most important emulation being Anṣārī's Persian book of the same name.[2] Both of these works emphasized "the importance of spiritual genealogy and lineage in establishing spiritual credibility and authority."[3]

Ahmet Karamustafa argues for a synthesis in Sulamī's writings between Sufi and Malāmatī elements. His allegiance to both trends is reflected differently in his various writings: the local Malāmatīs of Khurasan, of whom he was a member, and the urban Iraq-based Sufis, particularly Junayd's "socially conformist" school.[4] Shiblī, however, was by no means a social conformist, yet he is allocated a key role in the *Ṭabaqāt*, probably reflecting the importance of Shiblī's disciple Naṣrābādhī in initiating Sulamī into Sufism. In fact, there is an unusual connection to Shiblī in Sulamī's work, as Jawid Mojaddedi explains in his study of the Sufi biographical tradition: "The *Ṭabaqāt* also reveals a special interest in Shiblī, for, not only is his biography 'the head' of the fourth generation, but it is also the longest biography in the whole work by a considerable margin."[5].

Alexander Knysh argues that Sulamī has "the credit of preserving for us the precepts of a buoyant ascetic and mystical tradition [in Khurasan] that was eventually superseded by the Sufism of Iraqi origin."[6]. If this is the case, though perhaps Karamustafa's "synthesis" idea is preferable, then Shiblī is a key figure in this transition, both as being the master of Sulamī's master, Naṣrābādhī, and as giving credentials to Sulamī's Sufi, rather than purely Malāmatī, path. Shiblī's inclusion also broadened the limits of the tradition somewhat, from the "socially conformist" Junayd school and the Malāmatī movement.

Overall, Sulamī's importance for all later Sufi authors and the tradition itself cannot be overstated, particularly for his pioneering biographical works and his *tafsīr* writings.

Gerhard Böwering argues that Sulamī was "not an original author, but a compiler of Sūfī biographies, anecdotes and sayings, who copied his sources extensively, supplementing the materials with oral information."[7] He apparently collected his materials during his travels, especially to Marv, Baghdad, and Mecca. Böwering also argues that his work "documents the persistence of a significant esoteric vein among the Sūfī elite of the fourth/tenth century in coexistence with Sūfī works attempting a harmonization with orthodoxy."[8] In other words, Sarrāj's and Kalābādhī's attempts at harmonization were legitimizing a particular type of Sufi approach, with Kalābādhī not recognizing his own Khurasanian tradition around him, but "importing" the Iraqi-based school. Sulamī with his Malāmatī leanings, on the other hand, preserved this Khurasanian esoteric tradition, while integrating with the more esoteric Iraqi tradition represented by Shiblī's line.

Sulamī's work also illustrates the high degree of mobility and communication between Baghdad, Mecca, and Khurasan, as indeed does Kalābādhī's writings, given his even more remote location. Böwering also argues that Sulamī's "esotericism" included flexibility and openness to Shīʿite ideas, as documented by the position accorded to Jaʿfar al-Ṣādiq in his Qurʾān commentary.[9] The problem with this, however, is that the "comments" attributed to Jaʿfar are not specifically Shīʿite in character; though they are esoteric in nature, their Shīʿite quality is debatable to say the least.[10]

Johannes Pedersen, in the introduction to his edition of the *Ṭabaqāt,* argues for the now outdated view of the conflict between "orthodox" Islam and Sufism, with its climax in the execution of Ḥallāj. While acknowledging the developing science of *ʿilm al-taṣawwuf,* based on mystical experience and its psychology, to which Sulamī contributed, Pedersen simply states that Sarrāj was Sulamī's master, while Qushayrī was his student.[11] Such views are no longer tenable, given the arguments of Knysh and Karamustafa mentioned above.

Pedersen describes well the social and educational background of Sufi teaching reflected in the *Ṭabaqāt,* of *ḥadīth* transmission and the master-student circles that formed semiautonomously and more or less informally in mosques, the religious and educational centers of the day.[12] Prayer, discussion, spiritual exercises, lectures, and other forms of teaching and initiation were all carried out, for example, Shiblī being mentioned in the *Ṭabaqāt* as having a "circle" or place in the mosque at Medina.[13] This presumably reflects the situation during Shiblī's pilgrimage to the Ḥijāz. Shiblī is also mentioned as "converting" in the *majlis* (teaching circle) of Khayr al-Nassāj, and of extending his own *majlis* into his house.

Pedersen also argues for the importance of *ṣuḥba,* companionship between master and student, and their close rapport, meaning for example that transmitted sayings received their final form in *majlis* discussions, with responses formulated in a sharp and pointed way in the course of dialogue.[14]

Pedersen also notes the importance of oral transmission in the *isnād*s of Sulamī, the accuracy resting with the authority who transmitted the saying. Sulamī himself verified various traditions, for example, attesting to the accuracy of one of Shiblī's names from having seen it written on his tomb in Baghdad. This incidentally confirms his reverence for Shiblī as the master of his own master, by letting it be known that he visited his tomb. Pedersen also notes how many times Sulamī commences with "I have heard say . . ."[15] The problem is, however, that many of these *isnād*s are incomplete, particularly those of the earlier generations where one or two centuries are covered by only a few transmitters with obvious breaks in the chains of authorities.[16] Pedersen also notes various other problems with the *isnād*s, which need not concern us here. Interestingly, he notices the close correspondence between Sulamī and three later compilers, Abū Nuʿaym, Qushayrī, and Khaṭīb al-Baghdādī, all of whom we shall consider in later chapters.[17]

We are fortunate in having available two independent, well-edited critical editions of the *Ṭabaqāt*, which allow for some valuable comparisons. The texts of these two editions (by Nūr al-Dīn Sharība and Johannes Pedersen, respectively) show significant discrepancies, and some textual problems in either the early written or oral stages of transmission. Comparison of the two editions also shows the mutability of the text and the difficulty of trying to find the "original" or "definitive" wording for the various segments. This is an illustration of the flexibility of the tradition and also, on the other side, the elusiveness of ever claiming authenticity or primacy for its contents.

As is customary in each *Ṭabaqāt* chapter, Sulamī introduces his subject with a short biography, stating that Shiblī was Khurasanian in origin, from Usrūshana (or Ushrūsana), but as Sharība, an editor of the *Ṭabaqāt*, notes, the existence of such a town is doubtful.[18] Sulamī also states that Shiblī's birthplace was said to be Samarra in Iraq. It is stated that he "converted" to Sufism in the assembly of Khayr al-Nassāj, was a companion of Junayd, and was without equal in his generation as a person of spiritual experience (*ḥālan*), and in knowledge (*ʿilman*); he was also credited with being a jurist of the Mālikī school.[19] The remainder of the chapter is taken up with various sayings and verse attributed to Shiblī.

In a classic statement, echoing passages from Sarrāj's *Lumaʿ*, Shiblī is reported as saying, when asked about renunciation (*zuhd*), that it is "the turning of the heart from [regarding] things to [regarding] the Lord of things.' "[20] In a related way, he is also reported as saying "Inattentiveness [to God] for the blinking of an eye, for those who have intimate knowledge of Him, is associating others [*shirk*] with God."[21] Similarly, "Freedom is freedom of the heart from any other [occupation but God]."[22] Shiblī's pupil Naṣrābādhī is said to have heard him say "*Taṣawwuf* [the practice of the Sufi] is restraint of your senses, and consideration for your breaths."[23] This saying alludes to meditation techniques, the practice of *dhikr*, but also to the common Islamic concern of attentiveness to the transient and fleeting nature of life, one's limited number of breaths. Shiblī is also reported to have said that "One who knows God submits everything to Him, for He sees the vestiges of things' dominion in one";[24] "The world does not occur to my mind, for how can the world occur to the mind of one who knows the world's creator?"[25] Similarly, "How can unitive experience hold good for you as long as you clutch something as your possession, and as long as you eye things which fascinate you?"[26]

Shiblī is also reported as expressing his alienation from people and the world in general, and indeed his welcoming of social rejection. He said "If the world were to accept me as one who is part of it, this would be a misfortune for me, but since their drink is not my drink, and their taste [*dhawq*] not my taste, they would not accept me."[27] These are the words of an outsider, someone who rejects the world, and who welcomes estrangement. In a similar way, he is reported as saying "People love You for Your favour and benefits, but I love You for Your tribulations" (addressing God);[28] and "From where comes my 'where'? I am as You see me; I live without heart and strive without purpose."[29] A further quote from the *Ṭabaqāt* illustrates Shiblī's outspoken style. Abū Bakr al-Rāzī reports hearing him say, "How the people need intoxication!" Rāzī asks, "My master, what sort of intoxication?" Shiblī replies, "Intoxication that they have no need of regarding themselves, or their actions, or their spiritual states," after which he recited some verse.[30] This "intoxication" is of course the intoxication of mystical experience (*ḥāl* or *waqt*) which, analogous to the drunkenness of wine, induces forgetfulness of self, but also "absent"-mindedness, or nonintentional consciousness.[31]

Some of Shiblī's reported sayings have a stream-of-consciousness quality to them, and appear almost as inspired, ecstatic expressions known technically as *shaṭḥ*. A few examples illustrate this: he said "God has turned a blind eye to me, and does not see in me the vestiges of His power; so I am one of the vestiges of His power, and one of the evidences of His might. Indeed I have been abased,[32] so that He has made strong every humility by my humility, and I have become strong so that no one is made strong (or boasts) except by me or by one whom I make strong. Nor are we separated, for how can we be separated when there has not come upon us ever the state of unitive composure?"[33] Again someone asked Shiblī, "Can the one seeking knowledge be assured of what becomes evident to him?" Shiblī replied, "How can one be assured of something that is not fixed and enduring? Or how can one be confident of what is not visible? Or how can one sense what is hidden?[34] For He is the outward manifestation of the inward reality; the inner reality of the outward manifestation." Then he recited some verse.[35]

Jawid Mojaddedi, in his study of Sulamī's *Ṭabaqāt*, notes the attraction of this work for reconstructing the early history of Sufism. He also points out the danger of such an approach, which assumes the historical accuracy of these biographies. While there may certainly be accurate information among the segments preserved in Sulamī's work, it is rather their "continued relevance in the judgement of later generations that they had been preserved and transmitted."[36] Conversely, an indeterminable number of other segments have been lost, or were preserved in other works. Mojaddedi also argues that it is difficult to decide which segments are "authentic" and which are "spurious," or which are "original" as opposed to those shaped by later transmitters. It is better to appreciate the function of biographical works, serving as models of ideal belief and conduct, rather than searching for their historical accuracy.[37]

CHAPTER 6

Abū Nuʿaym's *Ornament of God's Friends*

A pupil of Sulamī, and of a younger generation, Abū Nuʿaym al-Iṣfahānī (948–1038) was a traditionist and biographical compiler. Growing up in a scholarly, religiously inclined milieu in Isfahan, his grandfather a noted Sufi and his father a traditionist, Abū Nuʿaym received a thorough education and traveled widely, seeking traditions from contemporary scholars, including Sulamī. His reputation as a *ḥadīth* transmitter spread widely and he attracted many students, but his career was rather curtailed by a factional dispute in Isfahan between Shāfiʿī and Ḥanbalī factions. Though not strictly a Shāfiʿī scholar, Abū Nuʿaym was critical of the Ḥanbalīs represented by another famous Isfahani traditionist, Muḥammad b. Isḥāq b. Manda (d. 1005). Abū Nuʿaym was denounced and expelled from the great mosque, his banishment persisting long after Ibn Manda's death. However, this rejection may have saved Abū Nuʿaym his life at the time of the massacre committed at the mosque by Masʿūd, son of Maḥmūd of Ghazna, after his conquest of Isfahan in 1029.[1]

His greatest work, *Ḥilyat al-awliyāʾ wa-ṭabaqāt al-aṣfiyāʾ* (Ornament of God's Friends and Generations of the Pure), is a massive ten-volume collection of biographical traditions, completed in 1031. Though ostensibly a history of Sufi luminaries, it is the book's tenth volume (in the Beirut edition) that contains most of the actual Sufi biographies. The first nine volumes deal with earlier pious men and women, starting with the first four caliphs and other Companions of the Prophet, as well as the founders of the law schools, other theologians and religious authorities. By this, Abū Nuʿaym sought to integrate Sufism into the mainstream piety of Islam, a goal similar to that of the earlier authors we have been considering. The compiler of the *Ḥilya* had a special relationship with Sulamī, being a pupil of his, and incorporating into his work biographies of most of the Sufis found in the *Ṭabaqāt*. Though Sulamī is often quoted, however, there is no extensive repetition in Abū Nuʿaym's work, as several other sources are used as well. In this he preserves many early traditions otherwise lost to us, and as Raif Khoury suggests, his work is complementary to Sulamī's, particularly with regard to the more remote first and second centuries of Islam.[2]

A traditionist by training, Abū Nuʿaym paid special attention to documenting the anecdotes and segments preserved, giving the complete *isnād* for most of his quotes. Alexander Knysh argues that the author "filtered" the available material to make it conform to his understanding of orthodoxy and propriety. His selective approach is part of an apologetic agenda that sought to remove objectionable or embarrassing elements, advising moderation and condemning excesses such as the doctrine of incarnation (*ḥulūl*). A notable absence in this regard is the biography of Ḥallāj.[3]

Both Jawid Mojaddedi and Ahmet Karamustafa point out that careful consideration of the *Ḥilya* suggests that it is not wholly authored by Abū Nuʿaym but rather seems to be the product of a teaching milieu based on oral transmission from Abū Nuʿaym to his students.[4]

Karamustafa suggests further that rather than the *Ḥilya* being a purely apologetic work, the inclusion of the early pious figures of Islam who can hardly be called Sufis or mystics was not to provide a pious genealogy for the latter. It was simply a record of Abū Nuʿaym's perspective, as a representative of the class of *ḥadīth* collectors and critics, on the history of Islamic piety. Moreover, the lines separating Sufis, traditionists, and renunciants were not rigid in the early eleventh century. It is more plausible to see Abū Nuʿaym as a *ḥadīth* transmitter who included Sufis in his traditionist vision of piety, and thus claimed them for himself, rather than seeing him as a Sufi who sought to justify his allegiance by constructing a pious genealogy for his fellow Sufis.[5]

Abū Nuʿaym begins his account of Shiblī with a customary ornamental passage of rhymed prose (*sajʿ*) extolling his virtues. Unlike Sulamī's *Ṭabaqāt*, there are no biographical notices such as birthplace, teachers, associates, or date of death. In keeping with his reputation as a traditionist, however, the author provides an *isnād* for each saying or anecdote of his subject.

There are two accounts in the *Ḥilya* of Shiblī's hospitalization. These segments do not provide much detail on the nature of his illness, but, as with Sarrāj's report, they provide the basis for later elaboration, such as that of pseudo-'Aṭṭār. On one occasion, Shiblī was reputedly visited in hospital by a vizier of the caliph al-Muqtadir (reg. 908–932), and the patient asks him: "What does your lord?" The vizier answers: "He decrees and executes in heaven." Shiblī replies with great wit: "I asked you about the lord whom you serve [i.e., the caliph], not the Lord whom you do not serve!" The vizier then spoke to an attendant on guard, and he (the vizier or the attendant?) said to Shiblī: "I heard you say when you were lucid that every righteous man [*ṣiddīq*] who does not perform a miracle is a liar. You are righteous, so what is your miracle?" Shiblī answered: "My miracle is that you set in opposition my thought in a lucid state with my thought in a drunken state, yet these two are nothing but what God wills."[6] One of the functions of this account is to show the lucidity of Shiblī's mind, and the profundity of his thought, despite his being locked away for apparent insanity and loss of rationality. His characteristic wit is also much in evidence in this encounter with the vizier. What is noteworthy is his claim that his reason and nonreason (his lucid and drunken states) are only as God wills.

Abū Nu'aym also mentions a short episode in which Shiblī refers to his hospitalization in the following way: "I entered the hospital several times and swallowed various medicines, but this only increased my madness."[7] Pseudo-'Aṭṭār in the *Tadhkirat al-awliyā'* expands on this theme by having Shiblī say to the hospital attendants who try to give him medicine: "Do not trouble yourselves, for my pain is not such as is relieved by medicines."[8]

In his lengthy biography of Shiblī—some eight and a half pages of twenty-five lines each in the Beirut edition—Abū Nu'aym inevitably repeats some segments from the *Kitāb al-luma'* and the *Ṭabaqāt al-ṣufīya*. Thus, we find Shiblī's views on the ineffability of *tawḥīd* in both *Luma'* p. 30 and *Ḥilya* p. 374. He expresses himself using rhetorical "chain" figures of speech, such as: "Creation gets lost in knowledge; knowledge gets lost in the Name; Name gets lost in the Essence."[9] A famous statement of his is repeated from Sulamī's *Ṭabaqāt*, his saying about renunciation, that it is the heart's turning away from (regarding) things toward (regarding) the Lord of things.[10] Similarly, Shiblī's exegesis of Qur'ān 50.37, as reported by Sarrāj (see chapter 3), is repeated by Abū Nu'aym.[11]

The existence of these repetitions allows us to ascertain the extent of "original" segments in the *Ḥilya,* and to conclude that most are in fact found here for the first time. This strengthens our view of the existence of a "pool" of traditions from which our authors only preserved a certain amount. The size of this original pool is difficult to judge, but it is unlikely that the sources available to us have exhausted its capacity.

In Abū Nuʿaym's account of Shiblī's death, there is the same motif found in the *Kitāb al-lumaʿ*, namely of his servant forgetting to perform the correct washing ritual of letting water run through Shiblī's beard.[12] An account not found in the earlier sources, however, is Shiblī's questioning why some companions have come to visit him on his deathbed. On hearing that they have come simply to visit, Shiblī taunts: "The dead have come to the bier of a living one!"[13] This episode is incorporated by pseudo-ʿAṭṭār into his lengthy account of Shiblī's death in the *Tadhkirat al-awliyāʾ*, where some of these earlier elements are greatly expanded.

~

Jawid Mojaddedi in his analysis of Abū Nuʿaym's work notes that the *Ḥilya* has been regarded by many historians as a rich source of narratives, with its biographies longer than other comparable works, and much that is not available before the eleventh century. Mojaddedi argues, however, that we should not see in this a trustworthy historical source. The length of the work means that there are numerous variants and differing accounts of the same events, which have perhaps been included because the original compilation was by several "authors," that is, students or scribes of Abū Nuʿaym. Thus, we cannot take for granted that these biographies are historically reliable; it is a superficial reading that does so, and one that betrays the dynamic traditions behind Abū Nuʿaym's remarkable achievement.[14]

CHAPTER 7

Qushayrī's *Treatise*

After Sulamī's *Ṭabaqāt* and Abū Nuʿaym's *Ḥilya*, both dedicated biographical works, we move to the famous and popular *Risāla* (Treatise or Epistle) of al-Qushayrī, a double-genre book containing both a biographical component and a large thematic treatise.

The author, Abu ʾl-Qāsim ʿAbd al-Karīm al-Qushayrī, was born in 986 in Ustuwā in Khurasan, and came to Nishapur on business matters as a young man. There he became a disciple of the Sufi master, Abū ʿAlī al-Daqqāq, who was in turn a disciple of Shiblī's disciple, Abu ʾl-Qāsim al-Naṣrābādhī. He also pursued religious studies, Shāfiʿī law and Ashʿarī theology, with the leading scholars of Nishapur and nearby Ṭūs. On Abū ʿAlī's death in 1015, he succeeded him as master of his *madrasa*, having earlier married Abū ʿAlī's daughter, Fāṭima.

During the sectarian rivalries that flared between the Ḥanafī and Ashʿarī-Shāfiʿī factions in Nishapur after about 1040, Qushayrī became involved in defending the orthodoxy of al-Ashʿarī. When the conflict turned violent in 1054, he was imprisoned for some weeks by his adversaries. Coming to Baghdad, he was appointed to teach *ḥadīth* in the caliph's palace. Returning to Khurasan, he settled in Ṭūs until the sectarian conflict in Nishapur was quelled by Niẓām al-Mulk after sultan Alp Arslan's accession in 1063. Qushayrī died in 1072 and was buried in his *madrasa* beside Abū ʿAlī al-Daqqāq.[1]

Apart from his most famous work the *Risāla*, completed in about 1046, Qushayrī is known for various religious writings, most notably an exhaustive mystical Qurʾān commentary.

The apologetic purpose of the *Risāla* is evident, and in this respect it follows the models of Sarrāj's *Lumaʿ* and Kalābādhī's *Taʿarruf*. Ahmet Karamustafa argues convincingly, however, that Qushayrī also attempts a melding of Sufi thought with the new tools of *kalām* and *fiqh*, "to develop a theologically and legally savvy form of Sufism."[2] Qushayrī is also basically a scholar, as his work demonstrates, and the "happy marriage between Sufism and legal-theological scholarship is the hallmark of the *Treatise*"[3] Again, it is the Iraqi-based school of mysticism that is championed by this work, the local Malāmatī movement being almost totally ignored.[4]

As mentioned above, the *Risāla* is a double-genre book, the biographical section relying on Sulamī's *Ṭabaqāt*, while the lengthier thematic component draws, not unexpectedly, on Sarrāj's *Kitāb al-lumaʿ*.[5] The biographies, some eighty-three in all, are usually very brief, that of Shiblī's being a mere ten lines in length, though some are longer. The biography of Shiblī is essentially a summary of what Sulamī records in his *Ṭabaqāt*, mentioning his origins, his upbringing in Baghdad, his companionship with Khayr al-Nassāj and Junayd, his adherence to the Mālikī school of law, and so on. The language and phraseology in both accounts is similar enough to indicate Qushayrī's dependence on Sulamī as his authority.[6] One difference, however, is Qushayrī's characterization of Shiblī as not only the master of his day in spirituality (*ḥālan*) and in knowledge (*ʿilman*), but also in *ẓarfan* (perhaps "wittiness" or "*esprit*").[7] The author of the *Risāla* also criticizes an aspect of Shiblī's behavior, namely, that as a novice his ascetic exertions went to extremes, including actions such as rubbing salt into his eyes to prevent sleep (mentioned in the *Lumaʿ*), and his overzealous devotions during Ramadan. Characteristically, in this criticism Qushayrī cites the authority of his master, Abū ʿAlī al-Daqqāq.[8]

Most of the references to Shiblī in the *Risāla* are contained in the thematic or "treatise" sections of the book. These sections are similar to Sarrāj's *Lumaʿ*, dealing first with Sufi terminology and concepts, and then with the various stages of the Sufi path and their accompanying themes. These chapters are introduced by the author with a minimum of editorial addition, as in the *Lumaʿ*, but with numerous appeals to the authority of Qushayrī's master, Abū ʿAlī. The number of anecdotes and narrative segments in these chapters is quite extensive, sourced, as in the *Lumaʿ*, from the large reservoir of biographical details and sayings of the early Sufis.

Qushayrī mentions several accounts of Shiblī's extreme asceticism, evidently without his approval, as noted above. One is a tradition that as a novice he used to flagellate himself with switches. Whenever "forgetfulness came into his heart" he would beat himself until the sticks broke, and then beat his hands and feet against a wall.[9] In a related way, Aḥmad b. Muqātil al-ʿAkkī (d. ?) is quoted as saying that he once found Shiblī plucking out his eyebrows with tweezers. On being questioned about this, Shiblī replied that "Reality [*al-ḥaqīqa*] is apparent to me, and I cannot bear it. It is thus: I bring pain upon myself that I might feel it and that [the Real] be hidden from me; but I do not experience the pain, and [the Real] is not hidden from me, and I cannot bear it!"[10] This expresses the overwhelming intensity of Shiblī's experience of "awe and intimacy" (*al-ḥayba wa-ʾl-uns*).

Qushayrī repeats Sarrāj's statement of Shiblī concerning the folly of speaking about the nature of *tawḥīd*. On this same subject, Qushayrī has Shiblī say: "Do you know why your unitary experience is not authentic? Because you seek it within yourself [rather than in God]."[11]

On the subject of knowledge about God, two sayings are noteworthy. At the beginning of the *Risāla*, Qushayrī introduces the thematic part of his book with a chapter titled "The Principles of Unitary Experience Among the Sufis." On the first page of this chapter, he quotes an allusive and profound saying of Shiblī's that "God is One, the One known before definitions [*ḥudūd*] and before letters [*ḥurūf*]. Praise be to Him! There is no limit [*ḥadd*] to His essence, and no letters to His speech!"[12] This clearly shows Shiblī's view on the vexed philosophical question as to which has primacy, language or experience; he maintains here that raw mystical experience is prior to conceptual and linguistic thought. Complementing the sayings on knowledge mentioned in chapter 3 from Sarrāj's *Lumaʿ* is the answer he gave when asked about *maʿrifa* (experiential or mystical knowledge): "The first of it is knowledge toward God Most High, and the last of it is infinite."[13]

SAYINGS ABOUT LOVE

On the subject of love—the devotee's attitude toward God—Shiblī has much to say; three examples deserve mention here.[14] He reportedly said: "Love is called *maḥabba* because it obliterates [*tamḥū*] from the heart everything other than the beloved [*maḥbūb*]."[15] This is not only an incisive and profound saying, but is also a delightful play on words characteristic of his style. What is of interest here, however, is that this saying is probably not originally Shiblī's. In the *Lumaʿ*, Sarrāj expresses an almost identical statement in a discussion about the superiority of the Prophet Muḥammad (*al-ḥabīb*, "beloved") over Abraham (*al-khalīl*, "friend"): "They say that friendship (*khulla*) is what penetrates (*yukhallilu*) the heart, and love (*maḥabba*) is what is in the kernel (*ḥabba*) of the heart, meaning the inmost heart, and love is called *maḥabba* because it obliterates anything else from the heart; so therefore *al-ḥabīb* is superior to *al-khalīl*ʾ.[16] The saying seems to have had a rather free history; after being attributed to Shiblī by Qushayrī it reappears elsewhere in the same form, such as in Hujwīrī's *Kashf al-maḥjūb*,[17] and in "ʿAṭṭār's *Tadhkirat al-awliyā*ʾ" where it is attributed to Abū ʿUthmān al-Ḥīrī, a contemporary of Junayd who died in Nishapur in 910.[18]

Another astute saying reported of Shiblī is that "Love means that you are jealous for the Beloved lest one like yourself love Him."[19]

An enigmatic saying on a related theme is that "The lover perishes if he remains silent, but the one seeking knowledge (*ʿārif*) perishes if he does not remain silent."[20] The editor of the edition of the *Risāla* used here comments on this: "he perishes from grief, for he cannot express all that God Most High has wrought in his heart; he may give expression to something he does not understand, and this would harm him."

ECSTATIC EXPRESSIONS

The final chapter of the *Risāla*'s thematic section is devoted to *samāʿ*, literally "listening," but more specifically the audition of poetry and music, and by extension the ecstasy evoked in listeners. I have written more thoroughly about *samāʿ* elsewhere,[21] but here I wish to survey Qushayrī's discussion of the subject in relation to Shiblī. In a general statement about the nature of *samāʿ*, Qushayrī quotes directly from Sarrāj's *Lumaʿ*,[22] in which Shiblī says: "Outwardly it is temptation, but inwardly it is admonition, so one who understands its symbolic meaning is allowed to listen to this admonition, otherwise he causes temptation and brings suffering upon himself."[23]

Hearing the recitation of the Qurʾān is a powerful means of inducing the altered state experience associated with *samāʿ*. A dialogue between Shiblī and a certain Abū ʿAlī al-Maghāzilī illustrates a typical question-and-answer format used in discussion of various topics. Qushayrī has lifted the dialogue from Sarrāj with some abbreviation and some textual alterations that provide clear evidence of written rather than oral transmission. Maghāzilī says to Shiblī: "Sometimes I hear a verse of God's Book which cautions me to abandon (earthly) things and shun the world; then I return to my ordinary state and the people around me, *and nothing remains of this (altered experience), and I am pushed back to my former state.*" Shiblī replied: "As for *what you hear from the Qur'ān* it attracts you to Him, and this is empathy and kindness to you from Him; and as for being brought back to yourself, this is His compassion for you, because it is not good for you to be devoid of His power and majesty in turning toward Him."[24] Qushayrī's omission of those parts of the dialogue indicated by italics is perhaps an abbreviation of what someone considered unnecessary, though conversely it is possible that the *Luma*ʿ text was added to by a later copyist. An important textual variant, however, is Sarrāj's "cautions me" (*fa-tuḥadhdhirunī*) compared with Qushayrī's "urges me" (*fa-taḥdūnī*), the similar orthography but not vocalization indicating a written, rather than oral, variant in the transmission of the text.[25]

The powerful impact of the Qur'ān's recitation on Shiblī was shown in an anecdote about his hearing a verse during the month of Ramadan, and his physical reactions and verbal repetitions, as recorded in the *Luma*ʿ.[26] This episode is lifted by Qushayrī almost word for word.[27] What is remarkable about Shiblī's response to hearing a verse of threatened punishment is his continuous repetition of the phrase: "Thus do lovers converse!" The seeming incongruity of this is partly explainable by his poetic instinct coming into play, casting himself as the tormented lover, with God as the willful Beloved. These motifs are familiar in Sufi, and secular love, poetry, even to the extent that the distraught lover craves exile and punishment from the beloved.[28]

"One has the impression that Shiblī was possessed of a most poetical psychic substance, a soul that was often as it were on the verge of poetry. . . ." These comments by Martin Lings ring true especially in relation to Shiblī's experience of *samā*ʿ.[29] Toward the end of this chapter of the *Risāla*, Qushayrī reports an anecdote not mentioned in other sources that has him in attendance at a recital soirée. He is so affected by what he hears of the performer (*qawwāl*) that he is transported into an ecstatic state while remaining seated. That he did not "rise up" according to custom is noted by those around him, and he later explained by means of impromptu verse:

For me there are two types of intoxication,
for my companions there is only one;
what is something very special for me
is only one for others.[30]

His claim of special status and unique experience is understandable, and in fact the apparent conceit involved is characteristic of his sayings on other occasions. His singular relationship with God, the lover-Beloved nexus, mentioned above, explains his lack of modesty.[31]

HOSPITALIZATION

Returning to one of the more well-known episodes of Shiblī's life, the visit of his friends to him in hospital, we find a fascinating insight into the mutation of oral traditions. Qushayrī offers two separate accounts of the visit of friends and Shiblī's throwing stones at them, both stories differing from each other and from the earlier account in Sarrāj's *Lumaʿ*.[32] These three versions are similar in general outline, but there are differences in the choice of language, which gives clear indication of the oral currency of the story. As an example of the variation in these three accounts, the tabulation below is instructive:

LUMAʿ (p. 50)	*RISĀLA A* (p. 186)	*RISĀLA B* (p. 325)
So he said:	And he was saying to them:	So he said:
"Liars!	"Liars!	
You claim	were you	"If you claim
affection for me	my friends [*aḥibbāʾī*]	my friendship
[*maḥabbatī*]	you would endure	[*maḥabbatī*]
but you cannot	my trials!"	then endure
endure my censure!"		my trials!"

The differences in these three texts is quite marked if viewed in their written form, but are understandable if seen as records of originally oral communications. Moreover, Qushayrī seems to have taken his two different accounts from separate sources, given the different contexts, without seeing a need for harmonization. The second account (*Risāla* B) has no mention of the friends fleeing when Shiblī throws stones at them, and has the addition of two lines of verse that he recited on the occasion.

This story also has a long history in Sufi writings, being retold by Ghazālī in his famous *Iḥyāʾ ʿulūm al-dīn* (Revival of the Religious Sciences) and by Rūmī in his *Mathnawī*, where the central character is the Egyptian Sufi, Dhu ʾl-Nūn (d. 860), rather than Shiblī.[33]

DEATH

With the traditions surrounding Shiblī's death, there is a common theme first occurring in Abū Nuʿaym's *Ḥilya*, resurfacing in the *Risāla*, and again in pseudo-ʿAṭṭār's *Tadhkirat al-awliyāʾ*. Each reappearance shows distinct variations, which again suggests oral circulation of these traditions. Abū Nuʿaym has Shiblī say on his deathbed: "I never gave a bribe, and I was not content without Him, and my reason became lost in Him"[34] This mention of a "bribe" recurs in the *Risāla* in somewhat different guise. Qushayrī relates that Shiblī was prompted to recite the *shahāda* ("There is no god but God") during his final hours, but instead recited two lines of verse:

> The Sultan said to his beloved:
> "I do not accept a bribe."
> So ask Him by His right,
> "Why do You stir up trouble by killing me?"[35]

This version from the *Risāla* reappears in changed form in pseudo-ʿAṭṭār's *Tadhkirat al-awliyāʾ*, neatly contextualized among other deathbed narratives. The author there abbreviates Shiblī's recitation to: "The Sultan of love says: I do not accept a bribe."[36]

We have noted above the dual-genre structure of Qushayrī's *Risāla*, its integration of biographical and thematic sections, and the author's mastery of both genres. That many later generations read, studied, translated, and held the book in high esteem, confirms the relevance and importance of this work, and the author's great contribution to the documentation of the Sufi tradition.[37]

CHAPTER 8

Hujwīrī's *Revealing the Veiled*

Contemporary with Qushayrī was the Persian-speaking scholar Abu ʾl-Ḥasan ʿAlī ibn ʿUthmān al-Jullābī al-Hujwīrī, whose only surviving work is the *Kashf al-maḥjūb* (Revealing the Veiled). Born in Ghazna, Hujwīrī traveled widely and spent his last days in Lahore, but we have few reliable details about his life apart from some ambiguous references found in his book.[1]

Hujwīrī seems to have had a traditional scholastic education with an emphasis on *kalām*, as suggested by his writings, particularly his desire to systematize teachings and "schools." His own teachers include the little known Abu ʾl-Faḍl al-Khuttalī, who was a pupil of Abu ʾl-Ḥasan al-Ḥuṣrī (d. 982), who in turn is connected to Shiblī and Junayd. Hujwīrī is thus in some ways a spiritual heir to Shiblī's vision of Sufism. The *Kashf al-maḥjūb* seems to have been written late in his life in Lahore, where he died sometime in the 1070s. His shrine is still a popular pilgrim destination.

At one point, Hujwīrī laments his being *giriftār* (either taken "captive" as a prisoner [so R. A. Nicholson], or else "preoccupied" [so Jawid Mojaddedi]) in the region of Hind, while writing his book. In the same sentence he complains that he cannot quote all the traditions of his own shaykh, because these written sources (*kutub*) are still in Ghazna.[2] His lack of a reference library has not substantially limited the value of the *Kashf*, however, for he seems to have had access to most of the works mentioned in our earlier discussions, or else a prodigious memory.[3] R. A. Nicholson notes that oral traditions were the main source for Hujwīrī's writing.[4] The other factor that compounds differences in both oral and written transmissions is that the author of the *Kashf* was writing in Persian, while most of his sources would have been transmitted in Arabic. Indeed, the *Kashf* is the first known Sufi treatise in Persian, and is thus an "original" composition drawing on the earlier Arabic sources.

Like the *Risāla*, the *Kashf* is a multifaceted work, with a substantial biographical section. It also contains a theoretical treatise of Sufi teachings, in which the author shows his expertise as a *kalām* scholar, and has discussions on more practical aspects of the Sufi way of life. Unlike the earlier works on which Hujwīrī draws, he is much more forthright in advancing and defending his own ideas, rather than simply presenting the teachings of the early Sufi masters without comment. This makes for a much livelier discussion in contrast to the more matter-of-fact writing of Sarrāj, Kalābādhī or Sulamī. The *Kashf* is divided into three main sections, first, a treatise on more abstract concepts such as the nature of knowledge, the meaning of *taṣawwuf*, and so on. The second section is mainly biographical, presented in chronological fashion, and reaching back to the Companions and Successors of the Prophet. The third section is a systematic elaboration of Sufi practice, including the inner meaning of the five pillars of Islam, and practical aspects of the spiritual path.

Ahmet Karamustafa observes that Hujwīrī tackles head on the problem of the diversity of perspectives on so many issues pertinent to Sufism. In an approach resembling the theological genre of doxography (*al-milal wa-ʾl-niḥal*), he organizes Sufis into twelve groupings, each named after a major figure representative of that viewpoint. These groupings are evidently artificial and somewhat arbitrary, but they allow the author to impose an order on a complicated array of views and subjects. Interestingly, he gave more coverage to the eastern Ḥanafī movement and the Malāmatī tendency than most of his predecessors. His ecumenical approach is another fusion of Sufism and legal-theological scholarship, like that of Qushayrī's *Risāla*.[5]

We have mentioned above that Hujwīrī drew upon many of the written sources discussed in our previous chapters. It was noted in chapter 4 that Kalābādhī writes of Shiblī as someone who "published" books and letters about the study of symbolism. Hujwīrī further alludes to the existence of other sources concerning Shiblī when he states, "I found [*yāftam*] in the anecdotes [*ḥikāyāt*] that one day Shiblī. . . ."[6] This almost incidental reference suggests, on balance, written rather than oral traditions; if it was the latter he would more likely have stated "I heard [*shanīdam*]. . . ." It also suggests that Hujwīrī searched out in libraries or other collections of sources for narrative materials dealing with Shiblī and perhaps other well-known Sufi figures.

Among the many biographies, or perhaps more accurately hagiographies, in Hujwīrī's work, Shiblī's "conversion" to the Sufi path and his noviciate under Khayr al-Nassāj and Junayd is mentioned briefly. The segment also contains an example of Shiblī's Qur᾿ān exegesis, and a single anecdote relating to his perceived insanity.[7] An interesting departure from the earlier Arabic biographical notices is Hujwīrī's statement that he was the son of the caliph's chief chamberlain. This attribution is only found in the Persian sources, notably Anṣārī's *Ṭabaqāt al-ṣūfīya* (see chapter 9); in suitably modified form—Shiblī being cast as an emir of Damāwand—in pseudo-ʿAṭṭār's *Tadhkirat al-awliyā᾿*; and, finally, in Jāmī's *Nafaḥāt al-uns*, repeating Anṣārī's tradition (see chapter 12).

The example of Qur᾿ānic exegesis referred to here is the one mentioned previously in Sarrāj's *Lumaʿ* (Qur᾿ān 24:30; see chapter 3). Characteristically, Hujwīrī elaborates further on Shiblī's brief exposition, with the dual "outer-inner" typology retained. The author of the *Kashf* quotes a further Qur᾿ānic verse (Qur᾿ān 17:72: "those who were blind in this life will be blind in the Hereafter. . . ."), and seamlessly links his comment that "the blind in this life are the sane and the heedless," with the following illustrative anecdote. Walking in the bazaar on one occasion, Shiblī was accosted by people saying: "Here is a madman [*majnūn*]!" He retorts: "You think I am mad, and I think you are sane, so may God increase my madness and your sanity!" Hujwīrī elaborates: "my madness comes from my intense love (of God), and your sanity comes from great heedlessness; thus may God increase my madness so that I grow ever nearer (to Him), and may God increase your sanity so that you grow ever further (from Him)."[8] This narrative is paradigmatic of Shiblī's character and ready wit. It assumes his notoriety among the general populace, and his known history of mental instability.

Hujwīrī inevitably repeats segments from the earlier sources, but often with some modification. An example is the report of Shiblī rubbing salt into his eyes to prevent sleep. The *Lumaʿ* mentions this practice, as well as the use of heated collyrium in the same way,[9] while Qushayrī also mentions the use of salt.[10] Hujwīrī conflates the two items referred to in the *Lumaʿ*, resulting in a rather awkward outcome: salt water applied by collyrium pencil or bodkin.[11]

In a different manner, Hujwīrī applies Sarrāj's paradigm of Shiblī's extravagance and wastefulness[12] by his having thrown 4,000 dinars into the Tigris and saying: "Stones in the water are better."[13]

Shiblī figures prominently in Hujwīrī's discussion of ritual purity and purification, a sizable section of the chapter on *ṭahāra* being devoted to anecdotes illustrating Shiblī's attitude.[14] Having purified himself, he was about to enter a mosque when he heard a voice from the unseen (*hātifī*) say: "You have washed your exterior, but where is your inner purity?" Shiblī relates that he turned back and gave away all his possessions and for a year wore only the clothes necessary for prayer. For this action he was congratulated by Junayd who said: "May God always keep you purified!" Shiblī thereafter strove to maintain constant ritual purity.[15] Hujwīrī then adds the well-known story of his servant forgetting to wash his beard when he was lying on his deathbed, as related by Sarrāj and Abū Nuʿaym (see chapters 3 and 6).

Shiblī's "hearing" a voice is a recurring motif, particularly in connection with his scrupulous purification and his entering the sacred domain of a mosque. Hujwīrī relates that once having purified himself, Shiblī prepared to enter a mosque, but a voice in his heart (*bi-sirr-ash nidāʾ*) assailed him: "Do you have such purity as to enter Our house with such boldness?" Hearing this, he turned back, but the voice said: "Do you turn back from Our door? Where will you go?" Shiblī cried out, but the voice continued: "Do you revile Us?" He stood silently in his place, but the voice said: "Do you pretend to endure Our affliction?" whereupon he cried out: "God, I implore You to help me against Yourself!"[16] The "voice in his heart" can be understood as the expression of an overscrupulous conscience, formed after years of ascetic training, questioning the purity of his motives and the probity of every action. In this present episode and the similar example mentioned above, the voice is doubtless meant to represent the promptings of the divine, the source of the conscience's scruples.

~

Hujwīrī's book combines the strengths of the treatise or textbook approach to Sufism with the biographical genre. Its "originality" as the first Persian work of its type is to be seen in the new material it adds to the biography of Shiblī, while preserving much of the earlier Arabic works on which it is based. Hujwīrī's skill lies in his deft integration of these new and old elements into a unified and coherent whole.

CHAPTER 9

Anṣārī's *Generations of the Sufis*

Following Hujwīrī, the next Persian author who is a source for Shiblī's biography is the Herat master, ʿAbdallāh Anṣārī (1006–1089). Anṣārī combined spiritual aspirations with the austere and conservative traditionalism of the Ḥanbalī school.

He began a traditional scholarly career early in life, adopting the Ḥanbalī way with enthusiasm, traveling to Nishapur, Ṭūs, and Baghdad for study, and later returning to settle in his native Herat. He was known as an orator and polemicist and spent a good deal of his time arguing against non-Ḥanbalī theologians, earning exile and imprisonment for his pains. Eventually triumphant, Anṣārī was able to preach freely to popular acclaim and honor in Herat. In about 1080–1081, he lost his eyesight and began to dictate his works, including an extensive Qurʾān commentary and books on Sufi subjects, such as *Manāzil al-sāʾirīn* (The Itinerants' Stages), which describes the ordered stages of the soul's journey toward God.[1]

Serge de Laugier de Beaurecueil, a modern authority on Anṣārī, writes that he "gives the impression of a strong personality endowed with exceptional talent and uncompromisingly faithful to the Hanbalite doctrine which he always defended with ardor. He was a spiritual master very much aware of the Sufi tradition but always personal in his judgements. Because of his education, Hanbalism and Sufism exist harmoniously in his mind rather than confronting each other."[2]

For our purposes, his most important work is the *Ṭabaqāt al-ṣūfīya* (Generations of the Sufis), in many ways a Persian adaptation of Sulamī's work of the same name. It is the earliest book of dedicated Sufi biographies written in Persian, following roughly the same generational scheme as Sulamī's compilation. As Jawid Mojaddedi points out, however, Anṣārī's method of arrangement follows slightly different principles from Sulamī's, such as grouping according to names.[3] Sulamī is honored by Anṣārī in being referred to as Shaykh al-Islām, and many of the segments begin with the formula "The Shaykh al-Islām said . . ."

Ahmet Karamustafa argues convincingly that Anṣārī was principally a pedagogue, a training master of disciples, whose narrations of the episodes from the early Sufis' lives served a larger pedagogical agenda. He did not share the academic outlook of many earlier authors such as Sulamī or Qushayrī. Moreover, his *Ṭabaqāt* "is a work rich in detail, and apart from the information it holds on Sufi history, Anṣārī's frank commentary also gives us access to his original and highly independent views on many early Sufis." For example, he declared Ruwaym b. Aḥmad (d. 915–916) and Abū Saʿīd al-Kharrāz (d. 890s) to be more important than Junayd, whom he considered too scholarly, and he reserved judgment on Ḥallāj.[4]

The *curriculum vitae* details of Shiblī—his name, birthplace, and so on—are largely based on Sulamī's *Ṭabaqāt*, though there is a curious anomaly here, namely, the statement that he was originally from Egypt. This sits strangely with other statements that he was originally from Usrūshana and was brought up in Samarra. Surprisingly, Anṣārī cites Sulamī as the source for claiming Egypt as Shiblī's birthplace.[5]

As mentioned above in connection with Hujwīrī, Anṣārī notes that Shiblī was the son of the caliph's chief chamberlain, a tradition peculiar to all the Persian sources.

A feature of Anṣārī's discussion of Shiblī is the tendency toward sanctification and hallowing of his subject. Thus, he quotes Junayd as saying: "Don't look on Shiblī with the eyes you look at each other, for he is an eye of the eyes of God."[6] Junayd is also quoted as saying: "Every people has a crown, and the crown of this people [the Sufis] is Shiblī'. Also from Junayd: "If you speak to Shiblī, speak to him from behind the heavenly Throne (*al-ʿarsh*), for his sword drips blood."[7] Such sayings have the effect of distancing Shiblī from ordinary human conduct and of sanctifying his persona. The process of making him into a saint—a *walī* or "friend of God"—is discernible in such statements.

Anṣārī makes the bald assertion that Shiblī was hospitalized twenty-two times during his life, with no other information given, or apparent connection to the surrounding segments. This seems to imply an assumed knowledge of his illnesses such that recounting them would be superfluous.

Finally, Anṣārī repeats the well-known saying of Junayd that Shiblī took knowledge that was heard only behind closed doors or in secret and divulged it to the public and in the mosque.[8] This renowned criticism of Junayd's is found recorded in the sources since at least the time of Kalābādhī, and is indicative of Junayd's caution and of his opposition to Shiblī's boldness and outspokenness.

Mojaddedi's analysis of the *Ṭabaqāt al-ṣūfīya* suggests that the work is a compilation by different "authors" or editors, something of a "school-text" associated with Anṣārī's circle of students and successors in Herat.[9] This does not really affect the way we value this text, however, and in the end it does not matter that our designation "Anṣārī" may mean the author himself or someone else from his school. What is more important for us is what is included and what is excluded of the segments and traditions surrounding Shiblī. It is noteworthy, and a little disconcerting, that relatively few segments of biography are included. Of those that are, few are concerned with his teachings or his characteristic deeds and known life events. It seems that the author(s) assumed a knowledge of the generalities of Shiblī's life and sayings, and that he (they) wanted to draw the reader's attention only to those narratives considered significant for some reason. Anṣārī or his school seemed eager to promote Shiblī's holy status, for example. It is, therefore, the case that we have a record of what Anṣārī deemed important about Shiblī, rather than a general view of his life and thought. While this qualification may well apply to all our sources, it is particularly pertinent to Anṣārī's book.

CHAPTER 10

Rūzbihān's *Explanation of Ecstatic Sayings*

A very different kind of source is the *Sharḥ-i shaṭḥīyāt* (Explanation of Ecstatic Sayings) of Rūzbihān Baqlī Shīrāzī. Not a biographical work in any sense of the term, the *Sharḥ* is an explanatory commentary on the sayings—not only the ecstatic ones—and the deeds of a number of the more outspoken and unconventional early Sufis, including Ḥallāj and Abū Yazīd al-Basṭāmī.

Rūzbihān's *Sharḥ* is an extraordinary work, in many ways the epitome of extravagant Persian theosophical mysticism. It is a work in which the author gives full rein to his exceptional imaginative faculty, as he "comments on"—or rather digresses to enormous lengths on—the *dicta* of the early Sufis. In the process he creates and gives sublime expression to a singular theosophical system that reflects much more on Rūzbihān than it gives light to the early Sufi masters.

Rūzbihān's vivid style mirrors his own experiences of dreams, visions, and ecstasies from his youth. Born in 1128 in the town of Pasā in the province of Fārs, he was raised without a religious education. Abandoning his trade as a greengrocer (hence, his name Baqlī), he joined a Sufi order, and traveled in search of religious knowledge. He settled in Shiraz, preaching in the mosque and establishing a *ribāṭ* (Sufi lodge) which continued under his descendants for several generations. He died in 1209.[1]

Among his varied writings are the *Kashf al-asrār* (Revealing the Secrets), a spiritual autobiography written in Arabic; a voluminous Qur'ān commentary also in Arabic; and the *Manṭiq al-asrār* (Language of Secrets), an Arabic forerunner of the Persian *Sharḥ-i shaṭḥīyāt* dealing with ecstatic sayings and their interpretation.[2]

Rūzbihān's usual format in the *Sharḥ* is to state briefly the act or saying under consideration, often directly translating into

Persian from the Arabic source, such as the *Luma*ʿ or *Risāla*. He then comments, expounds, and digresses to greater or lesser length, the size of each chapter thus formed being quite variable. Interspersed among these "explanations" are chapters devoted wholly to one or other concept or technical term that the author considers appropriate at that place.

In Rūzbihān's comments on Shiblī's ecstatic sayings, his writing is highly symbolic and allusive, "a prose style of great rhetorical density," as Carl Ernst describes it.[3] Consequently, we learn much more about Rūzbihān's thought than we do of Shiblī's motivations or intentions. The value of this, however, is that we find out about twelfth-century understandings of the words and deeds of Shiblī and the other early Sufis. These understandings are more symbolic, philosophically colored, and hallowed than those of earlier centuries, and are highly influential in the shaping of the hagiographic traditions of later generations.

Despite the usually florid character of Rūzbihān's writing, at times he clearly elucidates Shiblī's sayings, albeit on Rūzbihān's own terms. One example is a sustained discourse on Shiblī's saying that his companions have only interrupted periods of ecstatic experience (*awqāt*), whereas his are continuous, even infinite. Rūzbihān explains: "from [Shiblī's] deep drunkenness he says 'an eternal ecstasy and a sea without shore,' meaning 'my spirit is submerged in the sea of eternity, and that sea has become the source of my ecstatic experience; it has no limit; its shore is not part of the created world; limit and restriction have withdrawn from it.' The ecstatic experience of the one who knows God comes from the Real, and the Real does not restrict. . . ."[4]

Explaining Shiblī's actions of burning expensive clothes and putting amber under a donkey's tail, Rūzbihān says that these actions indicate the beginning of the path where one fears that desires may impede one from reaching the Real world: "In the scale of the love of these [renunciants] the world does not weigh a gnat."[5]

In explaining Shiblī's distributing large sums of money to everyone but neglecting his own hungry family, Rūzbihān repudiates the criticism of those who disapprove of his actions: "in the place of Majesty, taking and giving is by the permission of the Real."[6] He backs this up with verses from the Qur'ān, for example Qur'ān 2:245: "It is God who withholds and God who gives abundantly, and it is to Him that you will return."

On Shiblī's saying that asceticism is miserliness and pious observance (*wara*ʿ) infidelity, Rūzbihān argues that whoever looks on the world in a state of poverty and Sufi observance is niggardly, though he may speak of abandoning the world. Their secret regard for it is known to the Real: "all who are friends with the world the least little bit are niggardly."[7] As for pious observance being infidelity, Rūzbihān says that such people have tried to reach Unity by an intermediary, and thus are by Reality infidels: "all who imagine that by something other than the Real they can arrive at the Real, are ignorant of any knowledge."[8]

On Shiblī's saying that "the glance is infidelity, thought is associating others with God, and the sign is deception," Rūzbihān argues that "in Sufi terminology both the outer and the inner glance is by the secret eye, while the physical eye is occupied with the physical world; looking on other-than-the Real without remembrance or reflection is infidelity" (and likewise "thought" and "sign").[9]

Stylistically, Rūzbihān's *Sharḥ* is closer to the later hagiographical and theosophical tradition in Persian Sufism, the developments of the thirteenth century and beyond, shaped by Ibn ʿArabī's powerful influence. The more matter-of-fact compilations of the earlier Hujwīrī and Anṣārī seem rather pedestrian by comparison. In its hallowing of the early Sufi figures and its hagiographical approach, the *Sharḥ* complements ʿAṭṭār's *Tadhkirat al-awliyā*ʾ, which we shall consider in the next chapter.

CHAPTER 11

ʿAṭṭār's *Memoirs of God's Friends*

Coming to the most celebrated hagiography of Persian Sufism, the *Tadhkirat al-awliyā*ʾ (Memoirs of God's Friends) of Farīd al-Dīn ʿAṭṭār (d. 1220), we encounter a problem that has not arisen before. This is the question of the authenticity of Shiblī's "biography," which occurs in the appendix of ʿAṭṭār's work.

Some modern scholars argue that the original text contained only seventy-two "lives" of the early Sufis, ending with the cataclysmic career of Manṣūr al-Ḥallāj. However, several manuscripts of the *Tadhkirat al-awliyā*ʾ have an appendix containing later biographies, which include Shiblī's. The editor of the first critical edition of the text, R. A. Nicholson, accepted the appendix as authentic, while the translator A. J. Arberry considered only parts of this section to be genuine.[1] The editor of the more recent Iranian edition of the text, Muḥammad Esteʿlami, argues that the lack of this appendix in manuscripts earlier than the sixteenth century indicates that it is not authentic.[2] That both parts in Nicholson's view "are identical in method and style" indicates that if a later author is involved, he writes with essentially the same "mind" as ʿAṭṭār.[3] It is tempting to refer to the author of the appendix as pseudo ʿAṭṭār, as I have done in the present book, and while he may write in a similar manner to the original ʿAṭṭār, we must recognize the doubts about his authorship.

In view of this, the best procedure is to extract those narratives and sayings relating to Shiblī where they occur among the "genuine" seventy-two biographies, and to use material from the appendix for purposes of comparison only, as has been done in earlier chapters of this book.

The details of ʿAṭṭār's life are rather sketchy; we know that he lived most of his life in Nishapur and that he followed the profession of pharmacist/physician, but little is known about his teachers or associates on the Sufi path, or whether he was affiliated with a particular *ṭarīqa* (Sufi order). He was most likely killed by the Mongols during their bloody conquest of Nishapur in about 1220.

ʿAṭṭār is best known for his *mathnawīs*, or rhymed couplet epics dealing with various aspects of the Sufi path: the famous *Manṭiq al-ṭayr* (Conference of the Birds), and the *Muṣībat-nāma* (Book of Adversity), both allegories of the spiritual quest; the *Ilahī-nāma* (Divine Book) about a king and his six sons whom he tries to guide toward the religious life; and the *Asrār-nāma* (Book of Mysteries), a more philosophical didactic work. There are many other *mathnawīs* of doubtful authenticity attributed to ʿAṭṭār, as well as a genuine *Dīwān* of lyric poetry, and a collection of quatrains known as the *Mukhtār-nāma* (Book of Selections).

The *Tadhkirat al-awliyā*ʾ is the only prose work attributed to him, yet its language betrays the authorship of a poet, being sweet and fluent, as well as containing many fine examples of rhymed prose (*saj*ʿ). As for the "biographical," or more accurately "hagiographical," aspects of the work, Shahram Pazouki argues that "one will not find any biographies, in the strict sense of the term. . . . ʿAṭṭār does not merely compile facts about the shaykhs; he authors a work that recreates the spiritual world of the *awliyā*ʾ."[4] Similarly, Paul Losensky, commenting on the lack of source identification and chains of transmission writes that "ʿAṭṭār's purpose is primarily devotional, not historical, and he concentrates on the horizontal dimension of the text, its rhetorical persuasiveness and structural organization."[5] This devotional purpose of the work is reflected in ʿAṭṭār's own introduction where he lists the reasons for writing his "memoirs." He mentions that the deeds and sayings of the early Sufis are profitable and beneficial, effective in guiding one's own spiritual path, and may help to secure the friends' blessings on the reader.[6]

There is a standard structure for each hagiography in the book, namely an encomium in rhymed prose, usually followed by an account of the "conversion" of the friend in question, that is, their awakening or beginning on the Sufi path. This leads naturally into a section dealing with their noviciate and then the main section of anecdotes about the person's life and actions. This is followed by a selection of sayings, answers to questions, and words of wisdom attributed to the friend. Often the details surrounding their death are narrated, followed by accounts of their appearance to living people in dreams afterward.

What is most obvious about the *Tadhkirat al-awliyāʾ* is the greater distance in time from the period of its subjects who lived mostly in the eighth, ninth, or tenth centuries, and the consequent hallowing and sanctifying of their lives. This devotional character of the work is also most clear in the luxuriant growth of miracles and supernatural interventions in the lives of the early Sufis, factors encountered only rarely in the earlier sources. A related characteristic of the book is the greater detail and amplification it gives to earlier narratives, and the appearance of many anecdotes and sayings not found at all in the earlier sources. This may be accounted for partly by the loss to us of various sources used by ʿAṭṭār, as indeed he mentions the names of such books, either written by him or others.[7] Equally, however, this luxuriant growth of detail as well as the supernatural element is to be accounted for by pious accretion over the centuries; indeed, one of the great examples of this process is ʿAṭṭār's work itself. The devotional purpose and reverential attitude of the author should be kept in mind when approaching the *Tadhkirat al-awliyāʾ* from the distance of eight centuries. We must remember that the author was not writing to preserve biographical and historical details but rather to illustrate the patterns of saintly behavior, to provide a model for emulation, and to allow ordinary readers of the text to enter into the sacred domain of God's friends or "near ones" (the primary meaning of *awliyāʾ*).

SHIBLĪ IN THE SEVENTY-TWO AUTHENTIC CHAPTERS OF THE TADHKIRAT

As mentioned above, extracting the references to Shiblī from the authentic chapters is the most appropriate method of approach to ʿAṭṭār's work. In using this method, however, it must be remembered that Shiblī is not the primary player in these chapters and is often secondary or incidental to the action that centers around the main subject. This means that he may be portrayed in a less than flattering light, where his speech or behavior is sometimes seen as deserving censure.

An example of this is the earliest mention of Shiblī in the biography of Abū Ḥafṣ al-Ḥaddād (d. 878–879), a blacksmith of

Nishapur. According to ʿAṭṭār's account, Abū Ḥafṣ had connections with Junayd and the Baghdad Sufis as he traveled through Iraq to make the pilgrimage. Shiblī provided hospitality to Abū Ḥafṣ for four months, but despite his generosity—many different dishes and sweetmeats each day—he was mildly reprimanded for extravagance and wasted effort. Abū Ḥafṣ promised to show true generosity (*jawān-mardī*) to Shiblī if he visited Nishapur, and when he does so with a party of thirty-nine other companions, Abū Ḥafṣ lights forty-one lamps each night. Shiblī immediately accuses him of extravagance, so Abū Ḥafṣ challenges him to blow them all out. Shiblī makes a great effort but is able only to extinguish one of the lamps, the reason being that his host lit the forty in God's name for each of his guests, and one for himself. Abū Ḥafṣ triumphs over Shiblī by saying that what the latter did in Baghdad was extravagance, not this![8] The subtlety and wit of such narratives typifies the quality of ʿAṭṭār's writing, and makes the *Tadhkirat al-awliyāʾ* such an enjoyable book to read. A major difficulty with this episode, however, and one that illustrates the general problem of historicity in ʿAṭṭār, is a rather awkward chronological puzzle. Abū Ḥafṣ died in 878–879, sixty-seven years before Shiblī's death in 946, and allowing that Shiblī lived into his late eighties, this means that he was no older than about twenty years when the episode took place. Such youthfulness may explain Shiblī's lack of etiquette and manners, but it does not fit well with the received account of his conversion to Sufism later in life, at about the age of forty.

~

We are on firmer ground chronologically when we consider the relationship between Shiblī and Junayd, the latter dying in 910. The existence of one problematic episode, however, casts doubt on other more plausible accounts that are not obviously anachronistic.

Of the four narratives relating to Junayd, three cast Shiblī in a poor light, while the fourth is ambiguous. In the first episode, Shiblī states that if God gives him a choice of heaven or hell on Judgment Day, he would choose hell, for that would be the will or intention (*murād*) of the Friend, and doing what He wills is a sign of love. Such a statement is consistent with what we know of Shiblī's sayings, even his characteristic arrogance. However, Junayd surpasses Shiblī's statement by countering that he is acting childishly (*kūdakī mī kunad*), and if given an option, Junayd would not choose, for a servant has no choice.[9]

The second reference to Shiblī and Junayd in the *Tadhkirat al-awliyā*ʾ is directly taken from Qushayrī's *Risāla*. Shiblī is reported as saying, based on Qurʾān 18.39: "There is no power not [given] by God." Junayd replies that such words come from those who suffer "heartache" or "anguish" (*tang-dilī*), and this comes from postponing the feeling of contentment (*riḍā*ʾ) with what Destiny brings.[10]

In the third episode, ʿAṭṭār remarks with a gentle rebuke that Junayd's discourses on divine unity (*tawḥīd*) were often not understood by his listeners. On one occasion Shiblī uttered the divine name. Junayd immediately took him to task saying that if God was absent, mention of an absent is prohibited, while if He was present, mentioning His name during contemplation is irreverent.[11]

In the very last section of the chapter on Junayd, following accounts of his death, reference is made to Shiblī standing at his grave. On being asked for his thoughts, he does not directly answer but instead recites a line of poetry. He then says that the states of life and death are the same to the great masters. He expresses shame that in front of Junayd's dust he is "answering a question." that is, conversing with a mortal, and is ashamed of being in the state of life.[12] Shiblī here shows his great talent for witty expression, as he puns with the Arabic verbal root *ḥayya* "to live," which in its tenth verbal form means "to be ashamed."

These rather short accounts concerning Junayd and Shiblī give us a brief insight into their dynamic relationship. We know from the other source texts that their friendship was often a difficult one and that the master-disciple relation persisted perhaps until Junayd's death. The basis of tension was Junayd's "sober" and circumspect attitude contrasted with Shiblī's outspokenness and more unconventional behavior. Junayd was often berating his younger contemporary for his more "drunken" attitude, while Shiblī was always pushing the boundaries. These dynamics are illustrated in the first episode mentioned above, where Junayd speaks of Shiblī's "childishness" in pretending to "choose" what God wills on Judgment Day. This is consistent with Junayd's attitude toward his pupil, as in the second episode above, where he implies that Shiblī has an immature notion of accepting and being content with the divine decree. An indication of their relative positions is also seen in Junayd's upstaging and countering Shiblī's statements in the first three episodes above. The consistency of these accounts augurs well for the credibility of ʿAṭṭār's narratives. (See chapter 17 for a fuller discussion of their relationship.)

The next reference to Shiblī in the *Tadhkirat al-awliyā*ʾ is in relation to ʿAmrū b. ʿUthmān al-Makkī (d. 904), an associate of Junayd and a writer of letters and other documents, some of which are preserved in sources such as Sarrāj's *Kitāb al-luma*ʿ. In fact one of these short "letters" mentioned in the *Luma*ʿ provides an interesting comparison with the version found in ʿAṭṭār's book, the latter showing augmentation over more than two centuries of transmission. Sarrāj records a brief "letter," in fact no more than a sentence in length, by ʿAmrū b. ʿUthmān addressed to the Sufis of Baghdad. He writes: "You will never attain to the reality of the Real until you have traversed those paths which obliterate and those deserts which destroy." Junayd, Abū Muḥammad Jurayrī (d. 923–924) and Shiblī were present when this short document was read out. Junayd responded: "Would that I knew anyone who would enter such [paths]"; Jurayrī said: "Would that I knew anyone who would emerge from such [a journey]"; while Shiblī responded with: "If only I had the whiff of a scent of such [a journey]."[13] By the time this brief episode reaches ʿAṭṭār, it is considerably enlarged and enhanced with various details, presumably to add more color or more flesh to these bare bones. ʿAmrū b. ʿUthmān's single sentence is expanded into several, the "journey" being specified as the Pilgrimage, with a postscript detailing a spiritual pilgrimage through "2,000 fiery mountains and 2,000 stormy seas. . . ." At the end Junayd remarks: "Of these 2,000 fiery mountains I have crossed only one"; Jurayrī says: "I have not gone even three steps!"; while Shiblī laments: "I have not even seen the dust [of this journey] from afar!"[14] The elaboration of this episode from the "bare bones" of Sarrāj's account should alert us to what is at the same time the attractiveness of ʿAṭṭār's writing and his fallibility as a preserver of traditions. What began as a one-line statement with responses from three persons ended up as a half-page excursion with many added details. How difficult, then, is it to evaluate

ʿAṭṭār's narratives, for all their color and warmth, when we do not have many of the "originals" in an earlier source?

Shiblī is mentioned three times in relation to Abū ʾl-Ḥusayn al-Nūrī (d. 907–908), a colleague in Sufism, but of a much rosier, milder temperament than Shiblī. The first of these episodes concerns the arraignment of a group of Sufis, including Nūrī, Shiblī, and Junayd, before the caliph al-Muwaffaq (who ruled in lieu of al-Muʿtamid [reg. 870–892]). The Ḥanbalī prosecutor Ghulām Khalīl (d. 888) accused them of apostasy and, perhaps owing to political demands, the Sufis were speedily condemned to execution without proper trial. When the executioner summoned one of the companions, Nūrī jumped forward and offered himself in his place, impressing the authorities so much that a *qāḍī* was called in to adjudicate. He began to question the accused on points of law, and knowing Junayd was a proficient scholar, and having heard Nūrī speak, he decided to question Shiblī—"this mad or foolish tempered one (*īn dīwāna mizāj*)"—confident that he could not answer properly. To the *qādī*'s dismay, Shiblī answered intelligently and incisively, as did Nūrī when his turn came, responding so eloquently that the *qādī* was completely bewildered. He said to the caliph: "If these are apostates and unbelievers, I give judgement that there are no unitarians on the face of the earth!" The group was dismissed with honor, and the caliph was reduced to tears.[15]

This narrative as it appears in the *Tadhkirat al-awliyāʾ* is evidently based on a similar though shorter account in Abū Nuʿaym's *Ḥilya*.[16] Again we see the "bare bones" of the original, and the expanded version of ʿAṭṭār. There is no mention of Shiblī in the earlier account, and the questioning by the *qāḍī* is much briefer. The recurrence of the themes in this anecdote in different sources may indicate that Nūrī was summoned on several occasions before an inquisitor. Sarrāj, for example, has a chapter devoted to a range of indictments against Nūrī, mostly accusations of blasphemy, with his answers to these charges.[17] As Ahmet Karamustafa points out, however, "since our sources do not provide any social context, it is impossible to know if these [reports] were associated with real interrogations by political authorities in Baghdad or if they are to be viewed simply as narrative devices that grew around the one major trial of Baghdad Sufis in 264/877, though the latter scenario seems more plausible."[18] In fact, the date of this known trial does not augur well for a chronology involving Shiblī, since he would have been a mere teenager in 877, and hardly embarked on the Sufi path, which he seems to have begun at about age forty. The historical accuracy of such narratives must clearly be in question.

A second episode in the *Tadhkirat al-awliyā᾽* concerning Shiblī's relationship with Nūrī shows the latter in a superior role, almost acting out a master-novice dynamic. Nūrī enters a gathering where Shiblī is preaching, and accuses him of hypocrisy and not practicing what he preaches. Shiblī accepted the charge and retired to his house for four months without venturing out. A crowd of supporters eventually came and restored him to his pulpit. Nūrī heard of this and came a second time accusing him of concealing the truth, of being a veil between God and people. In the end he rebukes Shiblī as being *fażūlī,* "irrelevant" (so Arberry), or "an idle talker" or "busybody."[19] Such a narrative presumes more information on the relationship between these two than we have available. It assumes an underlying dynamic about which we know little, perhaps even an ongoing feud of some sort. The episode casts a poor light on Shiblī, who comes off second best in this "contest."

In a lighter vein, illustrating ʿAṭṭār's humor and delicacy, is a narrative in which Shiblī observes Nūrī's introspection (*murāqaba*). He asked him where he learned such excellent technique that not a hair of his body moved. Nūrī replied that he learned this from a cat sitting over a mouse's hole, and the cat was much stiller than he was![20]

Illustrating ʿAṭṭār's untrustworthy chronology is a narrative where Shiblī questions Yūsuf ibn Asbāṭ about humility and receives an appropriate reply.[21] Yūsuf appears in Qushayrī's *Risāla,* in connection with such ritual concepts as *tawāduʿ* (submissiveness), *waraʿ* (abstaining), and so on, but the problem with ʿAṭṭār's reference is that Ibn Asbāṭ died in 810, long before Shiblī was born. This underlines the problem of reliability in narratives for which we do not have an alternative corroborating source.

Shiblī appears several times in ʿAṭṭār's chapter on Ḥusayn ibn Manṣūr al-Ḥallāj, often illuminating the complex relationship between these two unconventional Sufis. ʿAṭṭār repeats a statement of Shiblī's concerning his connection to Ḥallāj already found in Hujwīrī's *Kashf*,[22] pertaining to a discussion of the legitimacy of Ḥallāj's thought. Shiblī is quoted as saying "Ḥallāj and I are of one disposition [*mashrab*, literally 'drink,' but Nicholson's text has *chīz* 'thing'], but madness [*dīwānagī*] was imputed to me; I found release, but Ḥusayn's reason [*ʿaql*] destroyed him."[23] ʿAṭṭār draws the same conclusion as Hujwīrī, commenting that "If he had been condemned, these two masters [Shiblī and Ibn Khafīf who likewise spoke in Ḥallāj's favor] would not have spoken thus in respect of him, and for us these two witnesses are sound."[24]

In Ḥallāj's protracted execution narrative, Shiblī appears in an ambiguous light as either supporter or opponent of the condemned man. ʿAṭṭār relates that he came up to Ḥallāj on the gallows and, quoting a Qurʾānic verse, asked him what Sufism is. Ḥallāj answered: "The least of it is this that you see," prompting the further question: "What is its greater part?" to which he replied: "You have no path to that." The crowd began to throw stones at Ḥallāj, and Shiblī, in conformity, threw a rose (*gulī* in Esteʿlami's text; Nicholson leaves the word unvocalized while Arberry reads *gilī* "clod" (of earth), an ambiguity only possible in Persian, not in Arabic). Ḥallāj sighed at Shiblī's action, and on being questioned, explains that the others who threw stones are ignorant and are excused for their actions; from Shiblī, however, the rose is painful, for he knows that he ought not to throw anything.[25]

It is related that after Ḥallāj's death Shiblī stood all night at his grave in prayer. At dawn he prayed a personal prayer asking God why He brought such suffering on a servant, one who was a believer, a seeker of knowledge and a unitarian. Sleep overcame him and he dreamed of Judgment Day, hearing a voice saying: "I did this to him in order to reveal Our mystery to other-than-Us."[26]

It is also related that Shiblī saw Ḥallāj after his death in a dream, and asked him how God judged those people who opposed or supported him. Ḥallāj replied that both groups were forgiven and shown mercy. It is noteworthy that Shiblī was the only named person to have a dream vision of Ḥallāj after his death recorded in the *Tadhkirat al-awliyā*ʾ. ʿAṭṭār recounts other people seeing Ḥallāj in this way, but they are anonymous, being designated simply as *buzurgī* "a great one/an important person." This shows the closeness between the two men, both as friends as well as in their outlook and thought.

It is with reluctance that one takes leave of ʿAṭṭār without considering the wonderful chapter devoted to Shiblī in the appendix to the book. Concerns about the authenticity of this addition must be heeded, however, irrespective of the attractiveness of the anecdotes it contains. The color and liveliness of pseudo-ʿAṭṭār's narratives about Shiblī are remarkable, particularly since many of the commonly accepted qualities of his personality are vividly portrayed in this chapter. One example is the character of his insanity and consequent hospitalization, which finds sympathetic expression in the *Tadhkirat al-awliyā*ʾ, with the integration of scattered references from the earlier source texts into a meaningful framework. Pseudo-ʿAṭṭār uses such motifs for literary purposes and with great skill to create a powerful narrative, in this way resembling the writing of the genuine ʿAṭṭār.

CHAPTER 12

Jāmī's *Breaths of Intimacy*

The final and latest Sufi source we are considering for the biography of Shiblī is ʿAbd al-Raḥmān Jāmī's (d. 1492) hagiographical compilation, *Nafaḥāt al-uns min ḥaḍarāt al-quds* (Breaths of Intimacy from the Sacred Presences), completed in about 1477. Jāmī was active as an author some three centuries after ʿAṭṭār, and such a late source as the *Nafaḥāt* is naturally dependent on the earlier works that we have discussed above.

Jāmī seems to have spent most of his life in Herat, near where he was born in 1414, and in the course of a traditional scholarly education he became deeply interested in Sufism. He became a disciple of the Naqshbandī master, Saʿd al-Dīn Muḥammad Kāshgharī (d. 1455), successor of the Naqshbandī founder, Bahāʾ al-Dīn. Jāmī seems to have lived a mostly quiet life as an author with a wide-ranging talent. His diverse and numerous writings testify to the flexibility of his genius, the depth and variety of his knowledge, and his perfect mastery of language and style.[1] He is probably best known as a poet, with three collections of lyric poems, and seven *mathnawī*s or rhymed couplet epics to his name. The *mathnawī*s, known collectively as the *Haft awrang* (Seven Thrones), include the popular *Yūsuf wa-Zulaykha,* a mystical interpretation of the life of the prophet Joseph, and *Laylā wa-Majnūn,* a romance based on the Arabic Majnūn legend.

Jāmī also wrote many prose works, including Qurʾān commentaries and interpretations of Ibn al-ʿArabī's *Fuṣūṣ al-ḥikam* (Bezels of Wisdom), and Ibn al-Fāriḍ's poetry. He also wrote standalone treatises such as *Lawāʾiḥ* (Illuminations), relying heavily on Ibn al-ʿArabī's mystical thought. His best-known prose work, however, is the *Nafaḥāt al-uns,* a collection of about 600 Sufi biographies from the eighth to the fifteenth centuries.

In his discussion of the *Nafaḥāt,* Jawid Mojaddedi points out that the "most immediately recognisable feature" of the sequence of biographies is its adoption of material directly from Anṣārī's *Ṭabaqāt al-ṣūfīya*.[2] One different aspect of the *Nafaḥāt*, however, is the grouping together of isolated biographies of Sufis with the same name. Mojaddedi observes that "the classification of early Sufis into separate generations had lost its relevance by the time of Jāmī's late fifteenth century re-structuring of the past."[3] This classification of eighth- to tenth-century biographies would have had much less significance for Jāmī than it would for his eleventh-century predecessors in Sufi historiography. Cl. Huart and H. Massé assert that Jāmī made use of ʿAṭṭār's *Tadhkirat al-awliyāʾ* while compiling the *Nafaḥāt*.[4] This is difficult to sustain, at least in the case of Shiblī's biography where few resemblances can be found, and in fact Mojaddedi disputes any influence at all in the whole work.[5]

As mentioned above, Jāmī includes much material from Anṣārī, whom he calls Shaykh al-Islām, but also from Sulamī. In fact he offers genealogies of Shiblī from both sources, despite some inconsistencies. For example, he quotes Anṣārī as saying that Shiblī was Egyptian and his father chief chamberlain. Jāmī also says that Shiblī was admitted to hospital twenty-two times in his life, again following Anṣārī.[6] This rather inflated figure concerning his hospitalization seems to be a recurring feature of the Persian hagiographies, with little support from the earlier Arabic sources.

Jāmī also records a rather novel account of Shiblī's death, which has little precedent in the earlier sources. The episode of the servant who forgot to wash Shiblī's beard is faithfully recounted, as found in the *Lumaʿ* and *Ḥilya*.[7] A further narrative is also presented on the authority of Bakīra (or Bakrān) Dīnawarī, the servant mentioned in Sarrāj's *Lumaʿ*. He reports that Shiblī had a premonition of his own death. They were walking to the mosque for Friday prayers when another man approached. Shiblī said: "Tomorrow I will have need of this man." Shiblī died that night and in the early morning Dīnawarī went to the house of the corpse washer who happened to be the man they had met in the street. He knocked on the door and the washer asked from inside: "Is Shiblī dead?" Dīnawarī was astounded, but the man reminded him of their meeting the day before.[8]

The existence of such a novel account in Jāmī's compilation suggests that he had access to different sources from those major ones we have already considered. It is one thing to have a slightly varying account, as we have seen in the works of previous authors above, but it is quite a different matter when a late source presents a wholly divergent narrative with no relation to any previous account. Apart from his having had access to different traditions not included elsewhere, another explanation for Jāmī's inclusion of this narrative would be his unwitting use of fabricated anecdotes that may have developed over the centuries, given the great chronological distance from the subject in question. The portentous element in this narrative adds to the suspicion that fabrication may have played a part here.

The death of Jāmī in 1492 has been claimed as the end of the classical period of Persian literature.[9] There was, of course, a continuing tradition, especially in the Indian subcontinent, but also in many other parts of the eastern Islamic world. As an original and creative writer in a long line of predecessors, Jāmī is a splendid example of the best, though not the last, of the Sufi hagiographical tradition.

In taking leave of the Sufi source writers, it must be noted that there are several other hagiographical compilations from the premodern period that we could have included. These later collections, however, tend often to be reworkings of the materials covered by the earlier sources that we have considered above. The present study is not intended to be exhaustive in its coverage, since this would become repetitive and unnecessarily lengthy. I have preferred to be selective and representative, giving the flavor of perhaps the most important and influential sources.

CHAPTER 13

Two Non-Sufi Historians

Khaṭīb al-Baghdādī and al-Dhahabī

Having surveyed a great variety of Sufi authors, biographers, and hagiographers, it is instructive to consider the viewpoint of some non-Sufi authors who mention Shiblī in the course of their writings. Their perspective allows us a more "balanced" view, or at least an outsider's observation of a Sufi personality like Shiblī.

As a non-Sufi historian writing little more than a century after Shiblī's death, Khaṭīb al-Baghdādī's (d. 1071) perspective is of great value. A historian of Baghdad, and a biographer of its noted scholars and others associated with the city's cultural and political life, Khaṭīb al-Baghdādī's fame rests on his biographical encyclopedia of more than 7,800 people connected with Baghdad in some way.

The *Ta'rīkh Baghdād*'s author is not strictly a religious historian with a particular doctrinal or ethical inclination, and his view of Shiblī is notably different from the other source writers we have considered previously. He notes that there are numerous narratives and anecdotes about him, and thus he has had to be highly selective in what he has chosen to include. This non-Sufi picture of Shiblī, from the following century, from the perspective of the cultural milieu of the great city of the empire, is a generous view. It notes his great piety and saintliness, rather than his dysfunctional/eccentric notoriety which became the image of later centuries.

The author does not mention Shiblī's unconventionality or mental instability, rather there is an emphasis on his religious credentials, his piety, and his generosity. Khaṭīb al-Baghdādī also notes his pithy sayings and expressive poetry, of which he offers several examples. He also illustrates through anecdotes his sound knowledge of Mālikī law, despite his unconventional behavior. For example, once while present with his associates or students in a mosque, Shiblī cries out and disturbs the surrounding circles of students and teachers. Annoyed, one of the neighbouring teachers tests Shiblī and tries to belittle him by asking an abstruse question of law. Shiblī answers brilliantly and shows himself not only in full command of his reason, but manages to put the questioner in the shade.[1] The author illustrates his scrupulousness in ritual washing for prayer on his deathbed, and also tells of his deep meditation and prayer, but also relates an anecdote about his compassion for the needs of a companion who is hungry, when Shiblī buys him some food in the marketplace.[2]

It is possible that Khaṭīb al-Baghdādī is showing a particular side of Shiblī for reasons not immediately apparent. We must remember that the author was in conflict with the Ḥanbalīs, and as a famed preacher and *ḥadīth* teacher he was accused of *taʿaṣṣub* (legal and theological bias), as well as falling foul of the Shīʿa during his stay in Damascus, which nearly cost him his life.[3] Khaṭīb al-Baghdādī seems to present Shiblī as a Mālikī scholar rather than a Sufi personality, given the emphasis on his piety but also his strict and exacting knowledge and practice of the *sharīʿa*. This seems to be the point of many of the segments chosen for inclusion.[4] Ibn Khallikān in his famous *Biographical Dictionary* also presents Shiblī as a pious Sufi, and as a follower of strict Mālikī law.[5] Khaṭīb al-Baghdādī also uses Sulamī as a source for Sufi biographies, quoted through intermediaries.[6]

The fourteenth-century Damascene traditionist and historian, Shams al-Dīn al-Dhahabī (d. 1348), aligned to the Shāfiʿī school, was a distinguished postclassical scholar, most famous for his extensive *Taʾrīkh al-Islām*, a comprehensive history of Islam beginning with the Prophet's genealogy and supplementing Ṭabarī's great work for the years after the latter's death. His writing was particularly important for the biographical notices, following the scheme for *ṭabaqāt* works, and having "far greater historical value than the general narrative has."[7] Because of its immense size, Dhahabī made several abridgements, some of which extract the biographical "classes" only, including the *Tadhkirat al-ḥuffāẓ* and the *Siyar aʿlām al-nubalāʾ* (Biographies of Distinguished Luminaries), published in some twenty-five volumes in the recent Beirut edition.

Ben Cheneb and J. de Somogyi note that like nearly all post-classical authors, Dhahabī was a compiler, "but his works are distinguished by careful composition and constant reference to his authorities."[8] For example, in his brief notice on Shiblī, he mentions Sulamī by name, and has obviously extracted material from the *Ṭabaqāt*, as well as from Khaṭīb al-Baghdādī's *Ta'rīkh Baghdād*. Nevertheless, Dhahabī makes some rather astute comments not found in the Sufi hagiographies. As a non-Sufi author, his importance, like Khaṭīb al-Baghdādī's, lies in his "outsider's" observations, for example, saying that Shiblī was a poet of keen expressions and maxims, and of spiritual experience and authority or capability (*tamakkun*). Then he writes that Shiblī would sometimes succumb to "dryness of mind" (*jafāf dimāgh*) and "intoxication," presumably meaning that his thinking was distracted and upset, and he would enter altered states of experience. Because of this he said things that required forbearance, as well as showing spiritual pride or boasting, which should not be emulated.[9]

A rather obscure saying, based on *Ta'rīkh Baghdād*, justifies his actions in burning clothes and other things, assuming knowledge of his behavior without actually recounting it. This makes the *Siyar* a supplement, as it assumes other biographical knowledge, whether oral or written.[10] Other episodes or anecdotes are obviously abbreviated from those found in the *Ta'rīkh Baghdād*, for example the commotion in the mosque where other teachers become annoyed at Shiblī's behavior and ask him obscure legal questions to try to humiliate him.

A further astute comment of Dhahabī is that Shiblī was "devoted to amorous and erotic poetry for which he had great sensitivity and taste; he also made amazing ascetic exertions which impaired his mental health."[11]

CHAPTER 14

Shiblī and the Sources

Conclusions

In considering the hagiographies of Shiblī, we have seen the complex interrelationships that exist among the different sources. It is not a simple matter of mere reworking of the earliest narratives by later compilers, but a much more sophisticated reinvention of structure and content to give a different characterization to the subject in question. The earliest source, Sarrāj's *Luma*ʿ, is not necessarily the basis for later compilers' work; Sulamī's eleventh-century *Ṭabaqāt*, being a dedicated biographical work, is a much more common model for subsequent authors. Conversely, the latest source, Jāmī's *Nafaḥāt*, includes new anecdotes not found previously, but evidently chosen from a larger "pool" of biographical material, some of which has not been preserved elsewhere. The reason for such elaborate interrelationships and the novel way each compiler arranged his work probably has to do with the different purposes and function of each hagiography within the community for which it was written. The selection of certain narratives, and which particular variants of those narratives, and the omission of others that could have been included, is based on the author's desired characterization of Shiblī. More than this, however, is the evolving mythology around a Sufi "saint" or "friend," which expands or ebbs with time, and colors his characterization. In Shiblī's case this involves, for example, his mental instability and hospitalization, not as significant in the earliest sources, but looming larger in the later Persian compilations.

Jawid Mojaddedi writes of these narratives being "creatively reworked through time," from the omission of seemingly insignificant details to the wholesale reshaping of segments giving a completely different characterization.[1] The accounts of the important figures in Sufi history have probably been reshaped the most, owing to their continued influence on later generations.[2] In our earliest sources, especially Sarrāj's *Lumaʿ*, Shiblī is accorded special status as one of the founding figures of early Sufi history. His impact on later generations was assured from the start, and thus we are left with divergent traditions about his life, which were shaped and reshaped by later authors.

Mojaddedi also asserts that most of the narratives in these hagiographical works originated in oral teaching and that they had undergone considerable transformation before their earliest appearance in written form. This accounts for the frequent occurrence of repetitions of similar anecdotes, sometimes with a simple change in the identity of the central character.[3] Examples of these variant narratives have been noted in the chapters above, confirming the importance of oral transmission and the prehistory of the written text.

SHIBLĪ: HISTORICAL SUFI OR HALLOWED SAINT?

It is inevitable that we ask the following questions when considering the different source texts that relate to Shiblī's life and sayings: How reliable are these accounts, and what historical weight can they bear? For the modern reader, at this remove, it is only natural that we wish to know the authenticity of the sources; it is part of our expectation as educated and critical inquirers that we can reasonably rely on the best documented accounts of his life. Did he really rub salt into his eyes to prevent sleep, or burn expensive clothes and perfumes, and all the other eccentricities attributed to him?

But no matter how pressing this "need to know" is for us, the fact remains that we are dealing with texts that have a religious and pious reason to exist first and foremost, where questions of "authenticity" or "historicity" are not answered in a way that satisfies our modern taste. Ultimately these modern questions are left unanswered, for the more we seek answers in the original sources, the more we are left with different models of emulation, with more examples of Shiblī's piety and asceticism, and further reasons for acknowledging his sainthood, rather than coming closer to the truth about his life events. As the sources for his biography multiply, so do the different approaches to his story, forged by different generations of followers or chroniclers with differing preoccupations and perspectives, and the needs of divergent communities to satisfy.

It is clear that our "historical" focus does not sit well with the pious character of most of these source texts. From the perspective of the writers of these sources, the question as to whether the events of his life are accurate or realistic in an historical sense is irrelevant as well as irreverent. The ultimate purpose of the writers of biographies and hagiographies is not to record facts, or even to throw light on their characters, but to conform to a paradigm of Sufi virtue and saintly conduct. Consciously or unconsciously, our source writers tell the life and death of the early Sufis in the way they want them to be understood. As Mojaddedi argues, rather than having our modern concern with historical realities, these authors were constantly re-creating the subjects of their compilations: "The perception of works of this genre by positivist historians as repositories of factual information therefore appears to be short-sighted and inappropriate."[4] Rather, the continual reshaping of past traditions was meant to reorient the models of emulation and authority for later generations, and to reinvigorate or translate into the present idiom the ideal actions and authoritative teachings of the past masters.

THE PRIORITY OF THE EARLIEST SOURCES?

On the face of it, if later chroniclers moulded Shiblī's story in different ways, this should lead us to assume that the earliest source, Sarrāj's *Lumaʿ*, would be the most truthful and reliable for the details of his life. Sarrāj was, after all, writing only just more than a generation following Shiblī's death, and it is reasonable to surmise that he would have most of the "facts" recorded accurately.

There are some problems to this line of reasoning, however, for proximity to the lifetime of the subject does not guarantee reliability. Often the greatest amount of fabrication occurs close to the original source of information, as family or followers seek to project the sanctity of their master. In the case of Sarrāj's selection of narratives and sayings, there is no assessment or justification of why particular segments were included, and why others were excluded. Many of the segments recorded first in Sarrāj do not occur in later source texts, while others appear in these later texts for the first time. The existence of a larger "pool" of biographical episodes explains the use of such material to illustrate or exemplify the theological and ethical propositions advanced by authors such as Sarrāj. From our perspective, the "arbitrary" nature of inclusion and exclusion of anecdotes does not augur well for our wish to gain a balanced and truthful portrait of our subject. The discovery of "new" segments in later sources also suggests the possibility of there being other texts containing valuable information that have been lost to us. It would seem reasonable to suppose that the sources we have today are neither the only ones that ever existed, nor necessarily the most important. For these reasons, the superiority of Sarrāj's *Lumaʿ* should not be assumed, no matter how convenient this would be.

Jawid Mojaddedi argues similarly regarding the status of Abū Nuʿaym's *Ḥilya*. This work has long been seen by historians as a rich source of biographical narratives, containing a larger number for each subject than other contemporary works, and many not found elsewhere before the eleventh century. One of the problems with the *Ḥilya*, however, is that competing and repeated segments of the same event occur often enough to cause logistical difficulties. It cannot be assumed, then, to be a worthwhile source of reliable historical information, without careful analysis and reconstruction.[5] In reporting the death of Junayd, for example, two different accounts point to the hazards of our finding out exactly how he died. Both of the accounts are plausible, and one cannot be accepted over the other. What is important, however, is that both versions have the same function, namely, the attribution of a pious death to Junayd, who is portrayed as persisting in acts of worship until his final moments. The significance of these accounts is thus in their function rather than in their historicity.[6]

LITERARY ASPECTS OF HAGIOGRAPHY

Other considerations should also signal caution in accepting these sources as factually reliable. First, it has been shown that it is sometimes difficult to distinguish between fictional and nonfictional modes of storytelling. This is pertinent to mixed-genre works such as Sarrāj's *Lumaʿ* where the author moves quickly through different styles of writing, from anecdote to biography to illustrative narrative to editorial comment, and so on. Historians and biographers were "not only transmitting and recording, but recasting—indeed, even inventing."[7] A related consideration is the question of "authorship," in our modern terms, of the sources used. Rather than being books with fixed contents more or less faithfully transmitted, many titles were students' or scholars' notebooks and copybooks, circulated among students and friends, and subject to all manner of alterations. Often these works would emerge only after the death of the reputed "author," and may not reflect his views adequately. Transmitters were not simply taking liberties with texts: they were *generating* the texts themselves.[8] In the case of Abū Nuʿaym's *Ḥilya*, for example, careful study of the text indicates that the reputed author was not solely responsible for its emergence. This huge work was the product of a teaching environment based on oral transmission from Abū Nuʿaym to his students, these latter contributing much to the final form of the work.[9] Allied to this is the fact that early Islam "valued the adaptation, redaction and reformulation of historical narrative, rather than the preservation of inert, historical data."[10] To see the early authorities as objective or reliable transmitters of Islam's origins, for example, or the early history of Sufism, is anachronistic, as it underestimates their creativity and their dynamism that made early Islam so adaptive and inventive.

In writing about Muslim biographers in general, Chase Robinson argues that they were interested not so much in what made their subjects unique as in what made them exemplary.[11] If character was not contingent and dynamic but determined and fixed, biography was not meant to explain human actions so much as to exemplify known truths and teach lessons by describing them.[12] This accounts for the frequency of "suspiciously similar incidents"[13] in the lives of the Sufis: the hagiographies were using paradigms, not writing individual biographies. Robinson also argues that the biographical process of creating an ideal character means that the philosophical and historical stance of the biographer, not the subject, dominates the composition of the work.[14]

Moreover, it is the fictional parts of the holy person's life that are often more valuable in literary terms. Not confined by "what really happened," they give free expression to "what ought to have happened." In this way there is greater conformity to literary or mythic norms of conduct that portray the ideal rather than the actual.[15] Alison Elliott, writing about Christian hagiography, maintains somewhat paradoxically that the more "fabulous" and less "historical" lives of saints show us more about the concerns of the author, and the literary tastes and motivating forces of the time.[16] Eric Ormsby remarks perceptively that "these accounts maintained a certain fabulous distance. The exemplary figure was enfolded within successive layers of tradition and reportage which both authenticated and haloed him. Dicta handed down by chains of transmission from one generation to the next had a hallowed lustre. The exemplary figure could be assimilated and internalized by pious emulation."[17]

In the case of Shiblī's hagiography in the appendix to ʿAṭṭār's *Tadhkirat al-awliyāʾ*, even if it was genuinely attributable to ʿAṭṭār, the colorful style of his writing would betray its greater fictional than factual quality. As we have argued above, we learn from hagiographies not a lot about the lives of God's friends, but much more about how they were remembered by later generations of followers and their chroniclers. In the end it is this representation that is the legacy that has come down to us. Hagiographers were not recording history "as it happened" (if this can ever be done), but were preserving models of faith for religious communities whose needs changed over time. The further away from the period of the "friend" in question, usually meant the greater the emulation—and the greater the hallowing of that special person. We can never really know whether such and such actually happened in Shiblī's life from the type of sources we have available, but we can know how he was seen by succeeding generations of chroniclers writing for particular faith communities. How his "life" was structured, and the way his sayings were arranged and edited, is important in showing the process of transmission of the saintly person's heritage for later generations.

THEMES AND RELATIONSHIPS

CHAPTER 15

Narrative Structures and Styles

In discussing the portrayal of the Abbasid caliph Manṣūr in the early historical works, Hugh Kennedy remarks that "medieval sources seldom discuss character in the way modern biographers would wish."[1] He acknowledges how difficult it is to reconstruct on the basis of scant evidence the character of someone who died more than a thousand years ago. Kennedy argues that in the case of Manṣūr, his portrayal is not "an extended description but rather a series of vignettes of short stories and anecdotes illustrating a quirky and difficult but at the same time very impressive personality."[2] This statement may well have been written about Shiblī: the sources may be different, but the way of writing history or hagiography in the Abbasid period is essentially the same.

The overall importance in these sources of the isolated anecdote, self-sufficient and transferable, has been stressed by scholars of both history and hagiography. For example, Ahmet Karamustafa, writing about the Sufi manuals and biographical works from the tenth century and later, remarks that "the fundamental building blocks of this body of writing were reports about individual Sufis, anecdotal in nature and normally transmitting a saying or a statement of the Sufi in question."[3] This "anecdotal atomism," as Louis Massignon describes early Arabic historiography,[4] is of course copied from the early science of *ḥadīth* which the Sufi manual writers and hagiographers esteemed and often emulated. Karamustafa argues that these anecdotal segments were compiled and reconfigured in various ways to serve different but related purposes: teaching of novices, pious remembrance, building confidence and solidarity among Sufi groups, and assertion against other rival groups.[5]

The inner structure of these anecdotal segments is often predictably similar, being formulaic, sometimes in a dialectical fashion.

Of three discernible types, the first and most elaborate begins with a setting or a particular circumstance, an action or statement by the subject, in our case, Shiblī. This prompts a questioner, often an associate or disciple, to ask for a meaning or explanation of the situation or topic prompted by the circumstance. The third part of this formula involves Shiblī's reply, stating his view or explanation, often in a pithy or witty manner, and sometimes with a sting in the tail.

The second type of structure for these anecdotes is simpler and more commonly found. Often without context, there is a question to Shiblī by an associate or disciple, or sometimes anonymously (Shiblī was asked about X), which prompts a reply or explanation, again with subtlety and wit. This "question-and-answer" structure is of course a traditional and time-honored method of teaching in an oral based environment, and very appropriate to the pedagogy of a Sufi master.

Perhaps we can see a third structural type with the addition of an *isnād* or "chain of transmission" to begin the anecdote. This listing of the names of the transmitting authorities, each having "heard" the anecdote from someone older who "heard" from another, and so on back to the one who "heard" or witnessed Shiblī himself, is a means not only of emulating the prestigious structure of *ḥadīth*s, but also of attempting to verify the truthfulness of the anecdote, given the authority and trustworthiness of the transmitters. It is notable that both Sulamī and Abū Nuʿaym, hagiographers who were by training and inclination *ḥadīth* scholars also, almost invariably include a full or partial *isnād* at the beginning of each segment. Other authors used the *isnād* form less assiduously, like Sarrāj or Qushayrī, and still others hardly at all.

The structural similarities of anecdotes made for easier memorization in an oral-based culture, and also for simpler compilation when they came to be written down. This ease of use also led to some pitfalls, however. Sometimes we find repetition or doublets of slightly varying material concerning the one incident or person. What is more worrying is that occasionally the same anecdote is repeated concerning two different Sufi personalities. Jawid Mojaddedi remarks about Sulamī's *Ṭabaqat* that "The inclusion of variant segments in the same biography, and, perhaps even more so in different biographies as utterances attributed to different individuals, highlights the hazards of treating a work like the *Ṭabaqat al-Ṣūfiyya* as a source of historical facts."[6]

The oral basis of many of these anecdotes also shows itself in the fictional character of their context. At times it seems that the wise saying of the Sufi master, the basis of the anecdote, is "the tail that wags the dog." A saying that originally circulated separately would come to "require" a context or occasion that (fictitious) embellishment would provide. Hence, the problem mentioned above of variants concerning the same or even different individuals.

The formulaic nature of these anecdotes is also evident in the repetition of specific situations or contextual frameworks into which different stories are inserted. For example, there are multiple anecdotes concerning Nūrī's confrontation with religious and political authorities in Baghdad, specifically his being interrogated on being suspected of apostasy or blasphemy. In these narratives, Nūrī is always able to answer the religious or legal questions he is asked in a more than adequate fashion. Karamustafa argues that given the lack of social context for such narratives, we cannot tell whether they are based on real interrogations by the authorities, or if they are simply "narrative devices that grew around the one major trial of Baghdad Sufis in 264/877."[7] The latter possibility seems the more plausible. Nūrī is also, like Shiblī, known for his unconventional behavior, for example, that he threw the proceeds of a land sale into the Tigris River coin by coin. The fact that Shiblī is reported to have done the same is perhaps not surprising, but it is a warning that the historical basis of such reports cannot be assumed. A similar narrative device seems to be operating here as with the stories of Nūrī's interrogation.

Alison Elliott, in reference to Christian hagiography, makes a pertinent argument applicable to the Sufis, that hagiographers aren't concerned that narrators before them have used the same motifs and details, nor about repetitions in their own stories: "The reiteration of familiar events gives the tales both plausibility and immediate intelligibility." Accounts of martyrs or desert solitaries borrow freely from each other and have "the imprint of a shared narrative deep structure."[8] On the face of it, the early Christian hagiographers seem to have indulged in repetition and borrowing much more than their Muslim counterparts, but the same process was at work, a difference of degree rather than of kind.

CHAPTER 16

The Nature of Shiblī's Sayings

Many of the varied and distinctive sayings of Shiblī have been referred to in the earlier chapters of this book. They are a significant part of his legacy and give a real insight into his thought and beliefs.

Shiblī's sayings are well known in the Sufi literature for their wit, unconventionality, and profundity. Many of them are pointed and quick-witted expressions, sometimes outwardly paradoxical or even irrational-seeming, and with a playful quality. In one sense, these are the expression of his *junūn*, his *'folie'* (so Émile Dermenghem), and no doubt they are one of the factors in his being labeled as insane. Yet there is reason in his madness; they are not mere nonsensical utterances. In fact, it could be argued that many of these sayings are highly refined and crafted, premeditated utterances with profound import and insight. They express the "inexpressible" truths of mystical experience in a highly articulate and memorable way.

Annemarie Schimmel characterized Shiblī largely by the fame of his paradoxical sayings and the shock value these had on his audience. So, for example, Schimmel notes the jolting effect of his assertion: "Sufism is polytheism, because it is the guarding of the heart from the vision of the 'other,' and 'other' does not exist."[1] Rūzbihān Baqlī's twelfth-century commentary on many of Shiblī's sayings, the *Sharḥ-i shaṭḥīyāt*, is regarded by Schimmel as the classic explanation that became normative for the later Sufi tradition. Thus, for example, Shiblī's exclamation that hellfire "will not touch me, and I can easily extinguish it" is explained by Baqlī as a genuine mystical experience: those "drawn close to God are burnt by the fire of pre-eternal love so that it is for them that God ordered the fire to be 'cool and pleasant' [Sūra 21.69], as He did for Abraham."[2]

Shiblī's sayings are not all of the same quality, however, and I propose that there are at least three distinct types that can be discerned.

1. The first type includes those sayings that are often recorded as answers to a specific question or response to a given situation, and appear as spontaneous and not overly premeditated. Even in these rather matter-of-fact sayings, however, Shiblī's characteristic wit and profundity are often in evidence, and there is "premeditation" similar to those in the second category outlined below. Thus, being asked to define "piety" (*waraʿ*), Shiblī replies that it is to be heedful or cautious (*tatawarraʿa*) that your heart is not distracted from God for the twinkling of an eye.[3] This example illustrates his use of a word play, strictly a *tajnīs* or *jinās*, in his reply. Similarly, when once asked about the initial letter *b* in the *bismillah* expression ("in the name of God"), he answers that it signifies "souls, bodies and moving things subsist in/through [*bi-*] God, not through their own essences."[4] Kalābādhī records Shiblī saying in response to a question about renunciation (*zuhd*): "What value is there in something worth less than a gnat's wing (i.e., the world) that renunciation needs to be exercised with regard to it?"[5] The reference to the world being less than a gnat's wing alludes to a Qurʾānic verse and *ḥadīth* to that effect.

   It could be argued that many of these rather matter-of-fact sayings are premeditated and well crafted, and thus there is no fast boundary between this first category and the second:

2. This next type includes those sayings that are often formally similar to the first, that is, they are recorded as responses to particular questions or definitions of concepts. The difference here is that they are obviously premeditated and highly crafted, and are thus likely to be more memorable.

   For example, in speaking of *tawḥīd* (the experience of unity or oneness), Shiblī is reported to have said that one who apprehends the least mote of knowledge about *tawḥīd* becomes too weak to bear the weight of a bug or beetle because of the heaviness of the burden of knowledge. Similarly, one who comprehends a mote of knowledge about *tawḥīd* bears the heavens and the earth on a hair of their eyelid.[6] The studied nature of such sayings is apparent, as is the use of hyperbole and paradox. Profundity of thought and experience is also evident in the following examples: being asked about *tawakkul* (reliance on God), he responds: "That you should belong to God as if you did not exist and that God Most High should belong to you as if He never ceased to exist."[7] The macrocosm reflected in the microcosm features in the following saying: "I move toward the infinite, but I see only the finite, and I move to the right and to the left toward the infinite, but I see only the finite; then I return and see all of this in a hair of my little finger!"[8]

3. The third characteristic type of saying is the ecstatic utterance, known appropriately in Sufi terminology as an "overflowing" (*shaṭḥ*). This type of inspired expression is best known in the famous formulas of identification with the divine, such as Ḥallāj's "I am the Real/Truth" and Abū Yazīd al-Basṭāmī's "Glory be to me!" Many lesser and not so controversial sayings are also included as ecstatic utterances, the key being their inspired and emotive content, expressive of a heightened state of consciousness.

Carl Ernst, in his classic work on this subject, states that "The forms of these expressions are strange, yet they do not presuppose complete intoxication. The technical vocabulary of states and stages was developed so that the Sufis could converse among themselves about their experiences. *Shathiyat* also serve this purpose. They are utterances in the service of the spirit. These may be experimental in character and deliberately unconventional, and they refer to a wide range of experiences. . . . *Shath* in general is an expression of a spiritual state, and it stands in a relation of more or less immediacy to the original experience, but this immediacy does not on principle exclude a certain amount of analysis and reflection."[9]

Some ecstatic sayings appear in Shiblī's biography as true outbursts of inspired, almost involuntary utterances. An example is the anecdote of his praying in a mosque during the month of Ramadan. When he heard recited the Qur'ānic verse "If We pleased, We could take away what We have revealed to you" (Qur'ān 17:86), he cried out, turned pale, and began to tremble. He then began repeating over and over the phrase: "Thus do lovers converse!"[10] In this apparently involuntary state he casts himself as a rejected lover of God, interpreting the verse of threat as a personal communication to himself. Sarrāj reports that Shiblī would go into ecstasies on hearing secular verse as well as the words of the Qur'ān.[11] In one such state he is known to have said: "Oh, no-one except He knows what is in my heart!"[12] These and other examples have already been discussed in chapter 3 on Sarrāj[13].

A slightly different type of ecstatic utterance is that which does not involve complete "intoxication," as Ernst remarks, and contains deliberation or reflection. An example of this type is his remark on taking and eating a piece of bread from a person: "My base soul sought a piece of bread from me, and had I turned my inmost heart toward the heavenly Throne and Chair, it would certainly have been burned up!"[14] His heart having a trace of the eternal, to turn toward the created Throne as other-than-God would be an act of polytheism, and thus deserving of hellfire. But such explanations of these cryptic sayings are problematical to say the least, and are at best provisional. Indeed, this is the character of Sarrāj's detailed commentary on Shiblī's sayings.[15]

In another sentence he implores: "O God, if You know of any residue of other-than-You in me, then burn me up with Your fire—there is no God but You!"[16] As noted before, these are the words of an assiduous and fervent unitarian. Sarrāj comments wisely that such statements emanate from a transitory altered state; its being transitory is a grace from God, since if it was a permanent state, all religious, moral, and social laws and responsibilities would be rendered null and void.[17] This hints at the unreason implicit in such statements and their inherent anarchy, which is destructive of the social order.

A third type of articulate and deliberate ecstatic saying is more in conformity with the famous "identity" utterances of Ḥallāj and Basṭāmī. Thus, on one occasion it is recorded that he said farewell to some friends as if he were speaking from God: "Go! I am with you; wherever you may be you are in my care and protection!"[18] Sarrāj explains this again as his being overtaken by an altered state that strips away his identity and nullifies his ego in the experience of unity.

~

In general, many of these sayings are obscure; perhaps this is part of their profundity. Others have an almost Zen koan quality in their teasing and paradoxical character. Yet it is also true, as Ernst remarks, that "ecstasy does not necessarily imply obscurity and unintelligibility; there can as well be an ecstatic apprehension characterized by total clarity."[19] Moreover, Shiblī's paradoxical expressions, his verbal agility, wit, and subtle use of language point to his deep contemplation on the nature of the Real. He attempts to express that nature by inadequate human language, and does not seek to display wit and genius for its own sake.

Ernst points out, however, that these audacious and often hyperbolic utterances have their rhetorical basis in early pre-Islamic boasting contests (*mufākhara*), where poets would compete in lavishing praise on their own tribe, while heaping scorn on their opponents.[20] The similarities between these ancient rhetorical contests and the Sufis' own jostling for temporal or spiritual honors cannot be denied. Indeed, as we shall see in discussing Shiblī's poetry, he was not averse to boasting of his own asceticism and spiritual attainments in rather immodest terms.

~

A final remark concerns the hypothetical question of the suppression or censorship of those sayings that collectors like Sarrāj considered too outrageous to include. Ernst quotes Hellmut Ritter who wrote that "the expressions of the early Sufis are subjected to a severe censorship, which only permits that which is tolerable by appropriate interpretation."[21] While we can never know the real situation in this regard, it must be pointed out that Sarrāj goes to great lengths in trying to explain and "normalize" these difficult and potentially blasphemous sayings, sometimes with only limited success. Rather than raising objections against Sarrāj and the other authors for possibly censoring what may have been unpalatable, they deserve praise for having recorded so much for posterity, which allows us to understand something of these daring and risky sayings.

CHAPTER 17

Shiblī and Junayd

Understanding the relationship between Shiblī and Junayd is instrumental in forming a more rounded picture of the former. The contrast between the two could hardly be more stark: on the one hand, we have the "young Turk" Shiblī, an erratic disciple with an intense ascetic outlook and unconventional ways; on the other hand, we have the older, revered master, the center of the most influential circle or "school" of Sufis, conservative, prudent, and circumspect. Junayd was of an older generation, dying in 910, some thirty-six years before Shiblī, and twelve years before Ḥallāj's execution. If these latter represented the ecstatic or "drunken" wing of Sufism, Junayd represented the "sober" or conservative wing par excellence. His stature and influence was enormous; nearly every Sufi *silsila* (chain of authority or genealogy) is traced back to him, and he is universally regarded as the formative figure or codifier of Sunni mysticism.

Yet is this widely accepted view of Junayd's cautiousness and prudence really sustainable? Christopher Melchert suggests it would be foolish to oppose Junayd with Abū Yazīd al-Basṭāmī (or, by extension, Shiblī) as proponents of fundamentally different paths. Junayd admired both of these more outspoken Sufis and took them seriously. Melchert argues that it would be better to say that Junayd converted Abū Yazīd's (and hence also Shiblī's) mysticism into "something unthreatening to ascetics."[1] Junayd developed a language for describing mystical experience that was not offensive, partly because it was abstruse and not easy to penetrate. He also put a stress on outwardly acceptable behavior, and favored an inward direction for mystical activity, a style of piety that would not interfere with scholarly pursuits or family life.[2]

Shiblī may have come to reject or at least deviate from Junayd's version of Sufism; he seems to have grown far away from the prudent attitudes of his master. But Junayd's influence on Shiblī was nevertheless profound, perhaps unsurprisingly considering the many years of their association. Despite the many differences in their approach to the spiritual life, Shiblī seems to have regarded Junayd highly and with much deference. In fact it is these two aspects, their variant approaches and the respect shown to Junayd, which form the dominant framework for the many anecdotes found in the source texts. These narratives usually show a strained relationship, a clash of attitudes, with Junayd often disapproving of the actions of his younger disciple. Unfortunately, there is usually no detail as to what stage in Shiblī's career these encounters took place, but we can surmise from the contents that many came from the later part of his association, during Shiblī's maturity and relative independence. That he still deferred to his former master is indicative of the close bond between the pair, and the lasting influence of Junayd, despite Shiblī's divergence from the path of conventionality.

Sarrāj succinctly epitomises Junayd's attitude toward Shiblī with the following report: "I heard Abū ʿAmrū Ibn ʿAlwān say: I heard Junayd say: Shiblī is intoxicated; were he to recover from his drunkenness he would become a leader of great usefulness."[3]

The dynamics of their relationship is shown more fully in an extended passage in one of Sarrāj's chapters devoted to Shiblī.[4] The latter is reported to have said to Junayd: "Abū Qāsim, what would you say about one who has God as his sufficiency in word and in reality?" Junayd replied to him: "Abū Bakr, between you and the best of men there are 10,000 stages in this question of yours, the first of which is the obliteration of what you have begun with!" Sarrāj goes on to explain what Junayd meant, that with his superior insight he feared the pretence of what Shiblī claimed, and that one who had God as his sufficiency would have no need to ask such a question.

Junayd is next reported as saying that if Shiblī went further than his present stage of proximity to God, he would become a leader (*imām*). This appears to be a variant on his statement reported above about Shiblī's intoxication, particularly since the same transmitter, Ibn ʿAlwān, is cited as the authority.

Sarrāj continues, again on Ibn ʿAlwān's authority, that sometimes Shiblī would ask Junayd a question which the latter would not answer. Instead he would express his concern for Shiblī's stability or constancy, seeing that his agitation, rashness, and passion were expressive of the spiritual state of novices rather than adepts. It is not clear from what stage of Shiblī's career these reports stem; if from early in his discipleship, Junayd's concern would be unusual, hence it is likely that such anecdotes would stem from Shiblī's maturity. If this is the case, it is noteworthy that he continued to approach Junayd with questions as though he were still a disciple.

Finally in this section, Shiblī is reported to have said that once Junayd asked him what was on his lips. He replied "God," to which Junayd responded: "Go, and may God preserve you!" Sarrāj explains that Junayd feared for Shiblī's safety, that if God did not preserve him when his mind turned to anything other than Him, his spiritual state would come under evil influence.[5]

In an earlier chapter of the *Lumaʿ* in which Sarrāj records various letters to and from Sufis, one example is from Shiblī to Junayd with a short reply from the latter.[6] Shiblī writes: "Abū Qāsim, what do you say about an advanced spiritual state which when it appears it overpowers and dazzles and then remains and becomes permanent; it effaces all things seen [by the heart] and those things revealed, makes dumb all tongues and erases any acquired knowledge. Were people to gather round a person experiencing this [for consolation], the person would only feel more alienated and outcast . . . ; the result is that he would be bound in chains and shackles, his reason would be overwhelmed and altered, reality would act contrary to reality, and people would become [as] a hobbling cord!" After a week's consideration, Junayd wrote back: "Abū Bakr, by God! by God! when we are in society we take the [divine] word and we *delight* in it [lit. inhale] and *embellish* it and speak about it in secret [lit. in cellars], but you come along and throw off all restraint! Between you and the best of people are a thousand stages, the first of which is to pass beyond what you have described."

There are several difficulties with this passage, not least being possible textual corruptions or at least rare usages. The two words in italics above are textually uncertain, being unpointed in some of the manuscripts, and Richard Gramlich in his German translation reads them differently from R. A. Nicholson's text.[7] The use of some uncommon words in this passage may simply be an example of Shiblī's poetically inspired prose, though some *nawādir* also occur in Junayd's reply. Despite these difficulties, Junayd's response became paradigmatic in later sources for his encounter with Shiblī. The formulaic "what we spoke of in secret you came and divulged in public" is used on several occasions as a standard rebuke by Junayd.

The common theme running through all the narratives recorded by Sarrāj is that Shiblī never really outgrew the master-disciple relationship with Junayd. It is perhaps a sociological given that such a relationship once formed is never broken, that even though the acolyte becomes a master in his own right, he still defers to his former shaykh. A further theme in these narratives is that Junayd saw Shiblī's turbulent spiritual state as a beginner's stage, an immaturity that needed much further development.

These same themes continue in the later sources, though there is also some variation and development. In Kalābādhī's *Taʿarruf*, for example, there is a shortened version of Junayd's reprimand for disclosing what the Sufis sought to keep secret. To this the author appends a rather enigmatic response from Shiblī: "I speak and I hear, and is there any other in the two worlds apart from me?"[8] As mentioned in an earlier discussion of this passage (see chapter 4 on Kalābādhī), pseudo-ʿAṭṭār in the *Tadhkirat* expands on this statement to the effect that Shiblī claims to be a mere mouthpiece or impassive medium for the divine message.

In Abū Nuʿaym's *Ḥiyat al-awliyā*ʾ the author preserves a rare statement by Junayd in which he compliments Shiblī's spiritual attainment. Junayd is reported to have said: "You are forbidden to say this to anyone, Abū Bakr, but the mass of people are drowned without God, while you are drowned in God."[9] Yet even here it is implied that Shiblī is known for his loose tongue, and the reference to his being "drowned" is allied to his "intoxication," of which Junayd disapproved.

In the chapter on "contentment" (*riḍā*ʾ) in his *Risāla*, Qushayrī reports Shiblī quoting to Junayd the *ḥadīth* (based on Qurʾan 18:39): "There is no power not [given] by God." Junayd comments: "This word of yours comes from a cramped heart, and that comes from abandoning contentment in what He decrees," whereupon Shiblī fell silent.[10] Junayd's insight into Shiblī's spiritual state is remarkable, for he does not disparage the *ḥadīth* itself, which may be superficially suggested by his reply. Rather, he penetrates to the discontent in Shiblī's heart, which caused him to utter this particular *ḥadīth*, one that is resorted to in times of distress.

In the Persian tradition, Anṣārī reports statements not encountered before in our sources. In four short pages in the edition used—most of these pages being taken up with footnotes—Junayd is mentioned some four times, more than any other authority. In a new departure, Junayd's statements about Shiblī are remarkably positive, for example, he is reported as saying: "Don't look on Shiblī with the eye you look at others, for he is an eye of the eyes of God."[11] Similarly, Junayd said: "Every people has a crown, and the crown of this people [the Sufis] is Shiblī." In a less flattering remark, Junayd is reported to have said: "If you speak to Shiblī, speak to him from behind the Throne [presumably, from a position of spiritual authority], for his sword drips blood,"[12] evidently a reference to his biting wit. Anṣārī also quotes the now familiar saying of Junayd that Shiblī took knowledge heard in secret and spread it abroad in public.[13]

Surprisingly, all these statements of Junayd in Anṣārī's text are made about Shiblī in the third person; there are no actual encounters recorded between the two. This casts some doubt on the authenticity of these reports, particularly since the majority occur in Anṣārī for the first time. That Shiblī is the "crown" of the Sufis, for example, is a universal statement that could well be attributed to many saintly figures in encomiums, such as those that begin every biographical notice in ʿAṭṭār's *Tadhkirat al-awliyāʾ*. The uncharacteristic generosity of most of Junayd's statements reported by Anṣārī also gives cause for concern about authenticity.

The biographical sources considered here largely agree in portraying, with great subtlety and succinctness, the complex relationship between Shiblī and Junayd. There is nearly always some degree of friction in their encounters, and Junayd mostly has the last word. In fact Shiblī is usually portrayed as the junior partner, deferring to his former master, while Junayd perceives the immaturity of Shiblī's spiritual states. Perhaps this situation is not really surprising, since, if the biographical data is to be heeded, Shiblī only entered the Sufi path at age forty, in about the year 900, while Junayd died in 910. This means that their association could only have lasted a decade, and that Shiblī was always a beginner in comparison with the maturity of Junayd. It is unfortunate that we have no information on the stages of Shiblī's career in which these encounters took place, yet the sources seem to suggest that he never really moved far from Junayd's orbit.

CHAPTER 18

Shiblī and Ḥallāj

Though there is less mention of the relationship between Ḥallāj and Shiblī in the biographical sources than between Junayd and Shiblī, the connection of these two unconventional mystics is crucially important. As Louis Massignon wrote: "The friendship between Hallaj and Shibli, in spite of their differences of temperament, was very great."[1] They were roughly the same age, and were kindred spirits as well as friends, sharing many of the same ideas and attitudes. But as destiny would have it, the two men took different paths in their quest for divine truth. For Ḥallāj, this path involved an "activist" stance, with preaching and involvement in religious and political causes, which in the eyes of some were the real motives behind his imprisonment and eventual execution as a troublemaker and provocateur. For Shiblī, his mental instability shackled his pretentions to renown as a preacher or charismatic champion, but in the end, it was probably his insanity that saved him from a similar fate to Ḥallāj.

Shiblī's relationship with Ḥallāj was not without danger: he was tainted by association and pursued for similar utterances. Pseudo-ʿAṭṭār writes: "He suffered much annoyance from the ignorant people of his generation; many accepted him, and many disapproved, and there was great commotion about him among the people who continually pursued him in order to destroy him as they did Ḥusayn Manṣūr [Ḥallāj], for some of his sayings had a likeness to Ḥallāj's'."[2] He apparently escaped Ḥallāj's fate because of his insanity, which alleviated responsibility for his words or actions. Hence, his famous saying, recorded first by Hujwīrī: "Ḥallāj and I are of one belief, but my madness saved me, while his intelligence destroyed him."[3] Richard Gramlich argues that in fact Shiblī was more astute or circumspect than Ḥallāj, knowing better when to remain silent. This idea is based on Khaṭīb al-Baghdādī's report, a variant of the one above, that he said: "I and Ḥusayn ibn Manṣūr are one and the same, only he spoke up while I kept silence."[4] In this way he showed his sense and intelligence, while Ḥallāj was perhaps more foolish and less cautious.

Gramlich also argues that Ḥallāj had "betrayed" the divine mysteries to an unworthy public. Thus ʿAṭṭār quotes, at the end of his hagiography of Ḥallāj, a report that Shiblī was at Ḥallāj's grave, and prayed asking God why he allowed his servant to be treated so badly. Answer comes that He did thus because he spoke "Our mystery" to others.[5] In some accounts, Shiblī accused Ḥallāj at his execution of this treachery, of having betrayed the divine mystery. In ʿAṭṭār's account of Ḥallāj's execution, this is ambiguously mentioned in Shiblī's reciting the Qurʾānic verse (Qurʾān 15:70): "Have we not forbidden thee all beings?" (Arberry's transl.). Shiblī then asks the dying Ḥallāj the meaning of Sufism, to which he replies that its least stage is this which you see. Shiblī continues and asks about its highest stage, to which Ḥallāj replies, "You have no path to that." ʿAṭṭār continues that everyone was throwing stones, and Shiblī, for the sake of conformity, threw a rose. Ḥallāj sighed when he felt the rose, explaining that the others were ignorant and are thus forgiven, while Shiblī knew that he ought not throw anything.[6] As for the Qurʾānic quote, which refers to the people of Sodom who accused Lot of interference and betrayal of their city, Massignon remarks: "Shibli's application of it to Hallaj is ambivalent: did he really betray his Sufi brothers by giving himself over to a public apostolate of mysticism, in opposition to the rule, held to by Islam, of not throwing pearls to swine? . . . Shibli, who was living the Qurʾan profoundly, utters this verse as a challenge. Has the time for divulging the secret come, since you may dare transgress the Law, so that it may execute you for having sworn that you received God Himself as your Guest?"[7] The basic problem with this view of Ḥallāj having betrayed the divine secret, or at least of his having divulged it, is that Shiblī himself was often accused, as we have seen by Junayd especially, of having done just this. How then can Shiblī condemn Ḥallāj of having done something with which he concurred and even applauded, and which he was often accused of doing himself?

Shiblī features prominently in the narratives and legends surrounding Ḥallāj's execution and final sayings. Not all of these anecdotes can be corroborated, however, and many must be fictitious and contain a large amount of legendary material.[8] Suffice it to say that Shiblī's prominence is a sign of his importance to Ḥallāj, and of their close friendship. Shiblī appears to have been forced to condemn Ḥallāj in the end, as the story of the rose indicates, but this can only be due to public pressure, "for the sake of conformity" as ʿAṭṭār puts it. He well knew, as could be seen with his own eyes, the price of unconventionality, and at this stage in his career at least, he was not prepared to cross the bounds and pay with his life as Ḥallāj was now doing. In fact, this pressure was part of Shiblī's great dilemma: how to express and communicate what was most urgent in his soul without falling foul of the authorities who had condemned Ḥallāj. Shiblī's answer to this problem was in his adoption of, or his falling into, insanity, which was the release valve of his existence. There was, for him, no other way of living with the divine mystery that so overwhelmed his spirit.

ʿAṭṭār relates that Shiblī saw Ḥallāj in a dream after he had died, and asked him what God had done to the two groups who had either supported or condemned him. Ḥallāj answers that God had mercy on them both; though his supporters knew what he was about, and his detractors did not know, yet both were excused or forgiven.[9] The historian Ibn ʿAsākir (d. 1176) reports from one Abū Bakr Zubayr (d. ?) who said, "I saw the Prophet in a dream and said to him: 'O Prophet of God, what do you think of Junayd?'—'He is the one who put (mystical) knowledge in order.'—'And what about Shibli?'—'When he was not in a trance, he was useful to many.'—'And Hallaj?'—'He was in too much of a hurry.' "[10]

CHAPTER 19

The Question of Shiblī's Insanity

"The radical behaviour of the religious virtuoso permits him closer contact with divinity and ultimately makes his divinization possible."[1]

The question of Shiblī's apparent insanity has been a point of contention since at least the eleventh century when it was first raised by Sufi authors. There is no doubt that his idiosyncratic behavior was regarded as rather strange by his contemporaries, as far as we can gather. But at what point does idiosyncrasy become madness, and is this not a label given by various parties to deal with difficult people?

Importantly, our earliest source, Sarrāj's *Lumaʿ*, devotes whole chapters to explaining and justifying his unusual behaviors and sayings, reconciling these to *sharīʿa* norms or common reason. Sarrāj has three chapters in which he attempts to explain and "normalize" Shiblī's actions, seeking to accommodate them and neutralize accusations of unconventionality. Evidently Sarrāj did not accept the notion of his madness, though it is perhaps another matter whether his chapters of apology are really convincing.

It seems that later generations did not share Sarrāj's conciliatory view of Shiblī's idiosyncrasies. Even today there is a range of arguments about his assumed insanity, as exemplified in Michael Dols's *Majnūn: The Madman in Medieval Islamic Society* (1992). Dols links and compares Shiblī's situation with Ḥallāj, and mentions Hujwīrī's famous quote of Shiblī that "Ḥallāj and I are of one belief, but my madness saved me, while his intelligence destroyed him."[2] In Dols's view, Shiblī's conduct was that of a "conventional" madman, allowing him to escape legal responsibilities, while Ḥallāj was unconventional but "sane" in his expression of ecstatic experience. Shiblī was an example of a holy man who feigned madness or was occasionally mentally disturbed, thus escaping persecution. Dols argues that Hujwīrī's report should be paraphrased that Shiblī's intelligence saved him but Ḥallāj's madness destroyed him. If Shiblī was genuinely deranged, he was not legally accountable for his behavior: "Madness was an excuse, perhaps the only possible excuse, for the unmeasured expressions of divine love and the unitive experience that the early Sufis were expected to conceal, while maintaining an esoteric prudence."[3] Dols goes on to describe Shiblī's behavior on the basis of the hagiography in the *Tadhkirat al-awliyā*ʾ, now thought to be by a later author than Farīd al-Dīn ʿAṭṭār.

The problem with Dols's assessment is that it is mostly based on the later Persian sources, notably Hujwīrī and pseudo-ʿAṭṭār. In the earliest sources from the tenth and early eleventh century, Shiblī's idiosyncratic behavior is mentioned, but not as overt insanity. Sarrāj, for example, briefly mentions his hospitalization, but it is the later eleventh-century sources such as Abū Nuʿaym and Hujwīrī who dwell on this. One must consider the likely embellishment at work in these later sources, and the full-blown account of his insanity is only found in pseudo-ʿAṭṭār from the thirteenth century or later.

A further consideration of Shiblī's insanity along the lines of Dols's is that of Florian Sobieroj in an important article discussing love and Shiblī's poetry. Sobieroj emphasizes the aspect of love for the divine that was such a feature of Shiblī's derangement, but he also points out his experience of periods of lucidity. People suffering from psychoses often enjoy lucid intervals, and for Shiblī this took the form of self-mockery or spiritual instruction, as Sobieroj notes. For example, Abū Nuʿaym in the *Ḥilya* reports him declaring: "You people of sanity. You have come to a Majnūn. What do you gain from me? For all the times I've been taken to the asylum and had medicinal potions poured into me, my madness has only increased!"[4] The well-known incident of his purported friends visiting him in hospital and his throwing stones at them to test their friendship also points to the deliberate pedagogy of his actions, rather than his derangement.

Another important but often overlooked consideration is mentioned briefly by Sobieroj, namely, the affirmative or positive aspect of Shiblī's mental unbalance. It is usually assumed that madness is unwelcome, destructive, and disabling, whereas for him the very opposite is the case. It is true that the prolonged psychosis described in pseudo-ʿAṭṭār is a debilitating illness, but again it must be stressed that this is a doubtful source, and this bizarre episode is not mentioned elsewhere, certainly not in any earlier accounts.[5] There is good evidence, on the other hand, that Shiblī welcomed the altered state of psychosis as "a positive state, while it is the 'sanity' of ordinary people which separates them from God."[6] For him it was a state of privileged spirituality and a means of drawing nearer to the divine presence. His insanity was perhaps involuntary in the sense that he had no control over its onset, and yet at the same time he welcomed and encouraged its arrival. This makes doubtful the notion that he "feigned" madness in order to escape persecution and responsibility for his actions. That he rejected everyday "sanity" is shown in Hujwīrī's anecdote that when he was once walking in the bazaar, he was accused of being a madman but retorted: "You think I am mad, and I think you are sensible: may God increase my madness and your sense!" Hujwīrī adds: "inasmuch as my madness is the result of intense love of God, while your sense is the result of great heedlessness, may God increase my madness in order that I may become nearer and nearer to Him. . . ."[7]

We should briefly consider the hostile and puzzling view of the famous Ḥallāj scholar, Louis Massignon. In writing about Shiblī's relationship with Ḥallāj, Massignon declares that "Shibli, for reasons of personal safety, preferred to assume the unbalanced gestures of a half-wit, to declaim his mystical truths in faked bursts of rhetoric."[8] This assessment contrasts with Massignon's view of Ḥallāj's nobility and his almost messianic suffering. It is strange that Shiblī's "insanity" should be judged so harshly and so easily dismissed when the related *junūn* of Ḥallāj is viewed so reverentially and empathetically by this great scholar.

A more charitable consideration is that of another French writing scholar, Émile Dermenghem, who writes that after Ḥallāj's death, Shiblī seemed to adopt the attitude of "a court jester in the service of the general public of believers." He came to express mystical truths capable of touching those for whom they were destined without being taken seriously by others and drawing hostile fire on those who were affected. By this ingenious "*folie*" he combined so dextrously the interests of esotericism, the need for prudence, and the freedoms of poetry.[9] With such virtuosity, Shiblī made use of a "folly," half-spontaneous, half-cultivated or affected, to teach with impunity his mystical truths by means of extravagant actions and words.[10]

Finally, the German scholar Richard Gramlich considers that for the everyday observer Shiblī was insane; cultured, witty, brilliant, pious, but insane. According to this world's standards he lived in another upside-down world; his conduct was often difficult to distinguish as it lay between insanity and deliberate or feigned madness.[11] The problem with this assessment, however, is that Shiblī did not live by this world's standards. His insanity was on a continuum with his intense piety, which meant that he did not inhabit a topsy-turvy world, but One world. Abū Nuʿaym preserves an anecdote about Shiblī in the asylum where he asks the caliph's envoy about his real master; the envoy came seeking a "wonder" but Shiblī responds to him by proclaiming the harmony of his "drunken" and "sober" states.[12] This undermines the "insanity" assumption in an important way: If he has harmony in both states, where is the problem? It is in others' perception, surely.

How then should we see Shiblī's unbalanced behavior? We should, I believe, be cautious of the later, more embellished sources, especially pseudo-ʿAṭṭār, on which much of the argument of his derangement is based. The best and more reliable source is Sarrāj's *Lumaʿ*, in which the author is at pains to reconcile and integrate his acknowledged eccentricities with his particular Sufi vision. Furthermore, and most importantly, it seems that Shiblī welcomed and fostered the altered state experience that others called insanity, for its spiritual benefit, and to further his journey on the inner path to the divine presence.

CHAPTER 20

Shiblī's Poetry

"The relationship between mysticism and poetry is necessarily enigmatic. Because the mystical experience is ineffable, mystical doctrine is approximate, mystical language allusive. And, so, mystics have often turned to poetry with its phonemic patterning and symbolic richness to speak of their experiences and beliefs."[1]

Shiblī's only literary "remains"—apart from the various records of his sayings—are a significant scattering of poetic fragments, no full-length *qaṣīdas* or other specific genre poems, but a large number of short verses, sometimes only a single *bayt* or couplet, which are preserved in several of the early Arabic sources. In 1967, these scattered pieces were collected together by Kāmil al-Shaybī to form a *Dīwān*, and published in Baghdad. The most frequent source for these poetic fragments is Sarrāj's *Lumaʿ*, though a number of other sources, some not considered in the present book, also contain verses from Shiblī.

In some ways it is problematical to scrutinise mostly isolated verses, at most three or four *bayts*, without the context of the full poem from which many of these fragments have been taken. On the other hand, it seems that Shiblī chose to express himself by means of these short verses, and most of them are comprehensible in their isolated state. These brief utterances, often like explosive outbursts of condensed symbolic or theosophic meaning, are reminiscent of the inspired ecstatic sayings or *shaṭḥiyāt* associated with many early Sufis such as Ḥallāj and Basṭāmī. Martin Lings remarks that "Shiblī is known to have been one of the most spiritually intoxicated of Sufis, and one has the impression that he lived as it were on the verge of poetry—whence the many single lines and couplets, both brilliant and profound, which flashed forth from him so spontaneously."[2]

Before entering our discussion of Shiblī's verse, however, it is instructive to consider Sarrāj's approach to Sufi poetry in general.

In fact, the very title of Sarrāj's chapter on this subject, chapter 92 in R. A. Nicholson's edition, is indicative of the author's conception of the significance of Sufi poetry. It is titled "A Chapter Concerning Their Poetry Dealing with the Inner Meanings of Their Psychological States and Their Symbolic Allusions."[3] This immediately sets the scene for a discussion of Sufi poetry, though Sarrāj mainly limits himself to a large number of verse quotations. The title also nicely justifies the use and importance of poetry among the Sufis, countering the opposition of conservative detractors who might point to its frivolity and licentiousness. Thus, Sarrāj underlines the spiritual qualities of poetry, its expression of the mystics' inner states, and its indication of the transcendent through symbolic and allusive language.

At the end of the chapter, Sarrāj again acts to counter opponents of poetry and also to acknowledge the difficulty and obscurity of some of this verse. He concludes: "These poems have difficulties in them as well as plain meanings, both subtle symbolic expressions and intricate spiritual meanings. So let one who looks into them consider them carefully so that they understand their intentions and their allusions, and that they not ascribe to their authors what is not appropriate. If one finds a difficulty which is not understood, search out an answer by questioning one who does understand, for to every situation there is an appropriate sentiment, and to every type of knowledge there are those who have mastered it. Were we to occupy ourselves with explaining this, our book would become too long."[4]

In his introduction to Shiblī's *Dīwān*, Kāmil al-Shaybī provides an excellent analysis of his poetry, its style and significance. Shaybī notes that Shiblī's verse is concerned only with his life as a Sufi, expressing his states and experiences in the second half of his life, finding voice for the full intensity of his experiences and beliefs.[5] It is perhaps not surprising that Shiblī only speaks of his present state and ignores his life before his "conversion" to the Sufi path, since his intense spiritual experience and its expression in poetry is much more important for him.

Shaybī argues that Shiblī went beyond the usual modes of poetic expression, from plain exoteric meanings to the extreme of spirituality, being inspired by what perplexed his spirit: "this is the difference between those who drift along behind a conventional life and those who make divine love their food and drink, clothing, sleeping and waking. . . . thus Shiblī and his like among Sufis stand in greater need of having a language filled with echoes and allusions which they use to express what is in their hearts of sentiments or thoughts, their 'overflowings,' the mere words of which are incapable of being carried to, and understood by, ordinary people."[6] In finding this incapacity of words, Shiblī makes use of the poetry of the pre-Islamic, as well as other Muslim, poets.

Shaybī emphasizes the part played by the early Arab tradition of the Laylā-Majnūn legends in Shiblī's poetry. This literary motif is important for his self-understanding and the psychological ramifications of the divine-human relationship. As with Ḥallāj and other Sufi poets before him, when asked about the beloved Laylā, the poet would respond with the self-referential "I am Laylā," taking the role of the distraught lover Majnūn, who identifies himself as one with his beloved.[7]

Shaybī outlines the complex nature of Shiblī's poetry, with its intertwining of three strands: "(i) a reflection of his psychological state . . . (ii) his cultural refinement, and (iii) his guidance for his disciples; thus it is multifaceted in its expression, meanings and purposes."[8] His poetry expresses first his inner state, the anguish and longing of his heart. Second the "meanings" are expressed in highly refined, allusive, and subtle language that taps into the huge reservoir of the Arabic poetic tradition. The third strand, the "purposes" and "guidance" mentioned by Shaybī, is the didactic thrust of his verse, the need to teach and instruct novices and disciples, sometimes taking the form of exhortation or giving counsel to his fellow Sufis. The versatility of Shiblī is also evident in his ability to dress his verse in the technical language of Sufism, to employ deftly the esoteric vocabulary in describing psychological states or alluding to spiritual matters. Another common feature of his poetry is a frequent reference to his distaste for feast days and celebrations, showing the extent of his ascetic disposition, and also a virtual "boasting" about his self-imposed austerities,[9]

Shaybī also notes that on various occasions Shiblī expresses an idea in prose, and then returns to it with an illustrative verse.[10] In such cases, however, the authenticity of either the poetry or the related prose should probably be questioned, since it is likely to be a situation of the tail wagging the dog. The appropriateness of a particular verse as an "illustration" of a prose narrative allows for the juxtaposition of the two, irrespective of their real connection and origins.

In terms of style, Shaybī argues that "Shiblī's expression does not fall outside the familiar (in poetic language), except when he comes to Sufism and its technical language. Nor is he given to meanings which entail difficulties of interpretation; rather, the mind and the pen alight upon them easily and smoothly; . . . they have a connection to the heart like that of perfume which diffuses in the air from fully opened blossoms."[11] Perhaps his style was not formally quite correct, however, as he sometimes uses repetition, which would not please a fastidious critic.

This mention of some "incorrect" stylistic features is reminiscent of the criticisms of Sufi poetry by some near-contemporary writers, notably ʿAbd al-Malik al-Thaʿālibī (d. 1038) and Abū al-Fatḥ ʿUthmān Ibn Jinnī (d. 1002). Th. Emil Homerin argues that these early Arabic literary critics identify certain linguistic and stylistic elements of verse associated with Islamic mystics. Thus, al-Thaʿālibī censures the famous poet al-Mutanabbī (d. 965) for "imitating the expressions of the Sufis and using their tangled words and abstruse meanings."[12] Without directly mentioning any examples, it seems that al-Thaʿālibī and Ibn Jinnī have in mind the uses of multiple and contrasting prepositions, repetition of a verb with different subjects, and the creation of paradox within a verse, among other stylistic faults.[13]

Some of these formal "errors" are apparent also in Shiblī's poetry, but as Homerin points out, such features are deliberate "plays on formal literary devices to induce a shift in perspective, to transcend rational abstractions to speak about nonrational concerns."[14] Shiblī, like Ḥallāj and many other Sufi poets, attempted to push the boundaries of language and meaning in trying to both understand their extraordinary experience and to allude to spiritual realities that were ultimately ineffable. That Shiblī's verse is nearly always richly meaningful is eloquent testimony to his linguistic and creative genius.

~

Shaybī gracefully states that "Shiblī's poems are constant in divine love, and these poems are truly among the most beautiful that his talent devised."[15] His sayings and verse dealing with the topic of love is the subject of a valuable article written by Florian Sobieroj in 1994, which is one of the few analyses of Shiblī's poetry.[16] Unfortunately, Sobieroj included in his discussion verse that Shaybī did not regard as authentic. Sobieroj does not mention their doubtful status, and I have disregarded these problematical poems in the discussion that follows.

An interesting and perhaps paradoxical adjunct to Shiblī's renowned asceticism is his apparent bodily corpulence, a rather unexpected outcome given his constant austerities. Sobieroj notes that this is not in keeping with the prototypical sufferer of love's affliction, who should in traditional fashion waste away. Perhaps Shiblī sought to justify his being overweight by claiming that his body was ignorant of the love in his heart:

> My heart loves, though my body does not know,
> for if it knew, it would not remain corpulent[17]

Despite the anguish of love's suffering, Shiblī expresses joy at annihilation in the Beloved, and if released from illness, he would call it back:

> I am delighted to perish in Him because
> I am overjoyed in what the lover delights in;
> and if my bones were asked about their torment
> they would certainly deny it, and you would hear
> the refusal;
> and if I was released from my illness, the fire of
> yearning in me
> would cry out, hoping for its return[18]

His fervent longing even had physical or psycho-somatic effects on him, as shown in a short couplet:

> Ardent longing for You has caused an ulcer
> to grow on my liver;
> my distraction for You makes me like
> a prisoner in fetters[19]

Sobieroj also notes that the recitation of these verses was accompanied by violent physical reactions. If love causes physical illness, it also has the effect of melting or dissolving his body from his heart and diverting him to the spiritual domain:

My body melted through what is in my heart,
and my heart melted from what is in my body;
cut my cord, or if You will, join it,
to me every deed of Yours is excellent;
people believe truly that I am in love,
but they do not know with whom I am in love![20]

Shiblī was not averse to quoting or slightly modifying lines from earlier poets. Sobieroj remarks on his interpretation of a quatrain from Dhū ʾl-Rumma (d. 735) describing the beloved's eyes. He expresses the thought that the lover has eyes in his heart that bring about intoxication:

As for the two eyes, God said: "Be!" and they were,
acting on the hearts [of lovers] as wine does.

This quote is recorded in Sarrāj's *Lumaʿ*, and is followed by a rare comment attributed to Shiblī: "I do not mean the wide eyes [of the face] but rather I refer to the eyes of hearts, within the breast; and happy is he who has an eye in his heart and an attentive ear and pleasing speech."[21]

Sobieroj's discussion centers on the theme of love in all its manifestations: ecstasy, illness, intoxication, madness; we will return to these aspects later. An important motif that occurs frequently, however, is the theme of asceticism and the question of celebrating religious festivals.

In several poems, Shiblī emphasizes the constancy of his proclaimed asceticism, which does not allow for the feasting and other celebrations of the festival days. Moreover, he makes a virtue of his unwillingness to celebrate, even to the point of boasting, and of vaunting his exceptional status: "they" have their festivals but "I" am alone in my patient vigil:

The people have fast-breaking and feast days,
I am solitary, alone, peerless[22]

The people rejoiced and were glad at the festival,
But I only rejoiced in Him, the One, the Eternal[23]

On festival day the people dress for the celebration,
but I have dressed in blue and black clothes;
I have prepared a lamentation and eulogy with weeping,
an antidote to the wine, sweet incense and aloes;
all have turned to joy at their feast day,
but I have gone among you with lamentation and eulogy;
I have turned to grief but the people are rejoicing:
what a difference between me and the people at
the feast day![24]

This air of superiority and almost self-glorification is perhaps a little odd given the humility most often associated with ascetic renunciation, but it shows a different side to Shiblī's personality. Such a boastful attitude is a constant danger that some ascetics, notably the *malāmatīya* (those seeking blame), were well aware of, and took steps to combat.[25]

In returning to the love poems, we may note that Martin Lings writes of "the state of spiritual expectancy, poised between longing and patience" epitomized in Shiblī's verse:

A cloud from You one day overshadowed us,
the lightning dazzled us but it held back its rain;
and its clouds did not clear so that one hoping might despair,
nor did its rain come that the thirsty might drink[26]

Lings argues that such statements represent an advanced stage on the spiritual path, that at the endpoint there are temporary "absences" of the Beloved: "when the soul resumes its earthly life it has a sense of separation, while remaining none the less aware of the supreme presence which it has not left and cannot leave."[27] Thus Shiblī says:

He saw me and kindled in me marvels of His grace;
I understood, and my heart melts in separation;
so He is not absent from me, though I seek consolation
in remembering Him,
and He does not turn away from me that I be absent[28]

Sobieroj expresses similar remarks in noting that "The correlative of union is separation, which in Shiblī's experience is preceded by the fear of being deserted by God. The fear for Shiblī was not of hell-fire, but that God might turn away from him."[29] Sobieroj quotes verses containing pairs of correlatives, a characteristic feature of Shiblī's poetry:

If separation were to settle in paradise,
  the grace of the garden would turn to hell for God's servants;
and if union were to settle in hell,
  the fire would turn to paradise for the servants[30]

Another type of paradoxical expression used by Shiblī, as alluded to above, is the Beloved causing illness and at the same time being the cure of the lover's pain:

My trials for You are such that
  I have no care for my hardships;
O cure of my illness,
  even though You are the cause![31]

Lings comments that this "inward sickness" so often mentioned by the Sufi poets is "the 'contradictory' condition of the relative that has been touched by the absolute, of the finite that has been opened to the infinite. The only cure is another touch, another opening. It is this 'sickness' which sets the adept apart from other men, and it is by its very nature a secret, since none can understand it except those who are smitten by it."[32]

In another example of the contrast between nearness and separation, Shiblī also uses the secular tradition of wine imagery to express intoxication and spiritual perception:

One who is accustomed to nearness does not endure absence from You patiently,
  nor does one whom love has enthralled cope with separation from You;
so take your time, wine-bringer, for the drink has already intoxicated me,
  for if the eye saw You not, then the heart has already perceived You[33]

Secular love imagery is also used in the following verses, the beloved (she) being an enchanter, her eyes making captive:

In her glances are flashes of sorcery,
by these she kills or brings to life whom she wishes;
and she makes captive the two worlds by her two eyes,
as though the two worlds were slaves to her;
I glance at her, and she knows what is in my heart,
I look at her, and she knows what I desire[34]

The image of the lover as a captive is also highlighted in the following couplets:

My limbs are not free of You for a moment,
they are ever occupied with carrying out Your wishes;
nothing comes to my tongue
—as God well knows—except remembrance of You;
and You are visible to my eye
—whether You are absent or present—it sees You[35]

Shiblī also uses imagery from nature with wit and a touch of humor, though his subject is ever serious:

Praise be to God that I am
like a frog that rests quietly in a lake;
when it croaks its mouth is filled,
else it is quiet and dies of grief[36]

The importance of spiritual perception is expressed in the following couplets:

When ecstasy [*wajd*] showed me Your presence
I witnessed Your existence [*mawjūd*] in every place;
so I declared Your existence without speaking,
and I saw Your certainty without seeing by the eye[37]

Finally, Martin Lings describes the following verses as "a serene expression of the permanent consciousness which the great mystic retains over and above any vicissitudes he may have to undergo:

Let the moons set or still be bright,
Ours is a full moon: in its sight
Full moons are humbled; for us its light
A splendour is by day and night.
No change of time can alter it"[38]

CHAPTER 21

Shiblī and the Qur'ān

For Shiblī and most other Sufi mystics of his time, the Qur'ān, its recitation, contemplation, and exegesis was a central part of their life and worship. As Alexander Knysh writes: "From the outset, the Qur'ān was the principal source of contemplation and inspiration for every serious Muslim ascetic and mystic."[1] As the revealed word of God it was not only the source of their faith and practice, providing rules and norms for every action, but it was also the primary source of their spiritual life, a guide for the inner journey and text for meditation and ritual recital.

Shiblī's Qur'ānic spirituality is shown in almost every anecdote and saying attributed to him. It is the guide and underlying motive discernible in his actions and speech, and the basis for his thought. Thus, we can trace back nearly every narrative about him to a particular Qur'ānic verse or injunction. In many ways it can be said that he tried to live the Qur'ān, to be an embodiment of the word of God as revealed to humankind.

As well as this living example, however, Shiblī bequeathed a considerable amount of formal exegesis and interpretation of individual Qur'ānic verses, which we shall consider in this chapter. These examples are found in the early Sufi *tafsīr* collections of Abū ʿAbd al-Raḥmān al-Sulamī, the noted tenth- through eleventh-century biographer and traditionist whom we have discussed above. Sulamī's *tafsīr* compilations, in particular his *Ḥaqā'iq al-tafsīr* (Realities of Exegesis) and *Ziyādāt ḥaqā'iq al-tafsīr* (Addenda to the Realities of Exegesis), preserve invaluable oral teachings and written works from Sufis of the eighth to the tenth centuries. These two works follow a verse by verse system, where comments attributed to early exegetes, particularly Ibn ʿAṭā', Junayd, Sahl al-Tustarī, and Jaʿfar al-Ṣādiq, stand side by side at the one verse.

Within this scheme of early Sufi *tafsīr*, Shiblī's contribution is significant, though he is not quoted very frequently. In many cases,

Shiblī gives an esoteric comment prompted by one or more significant words in the Qur'ānic text, on which he bases a discourse with more or less relevance to the context and setting of the holy text. Gerhard Böwering writes about this style of Sufi exegesis, known as the "way of allusions [*ishārāt*]," in the following terms: "These allusions are the result of the merger between Qur'ānic keynotes and the matrix of the Sūfī world of ideas. The keynotes, Qur'ānic words or phrases striking the Sūfī's mind, may be taken up in total isolation from the actual context. . . . Listening to the Qur'ānic word, the Sūfī is captured by a keynote, a fleeting touch of meaning communicated to him by the divine speaker. . . . With these keynotes the listener associates a cluster of images emerging from the content of his personal experience. These images merge with the Qur'ānic keynotes and find their expression in the allusions that are jotted down in the commentary in a condensed, abbreviated form. . . ."[2]

Occasionally, Shiblī uses a different methodology from this hermeneutic, for example, offering a quasi-philological approach where the keyword is explained etymologically, or with word play or repetition to emphasise and illustrate its significance. Only seldom is there reference to the context of the word or phrase being discussed, and instead there is often an anagogical interpretation offered, from the literal sense to a "spiritual" exegesis.

The following survey discusses a selection of *tafsīr* arranged in Qur'ānic verse order, to give a sample of his exegetical method.

In an extended collection of various *tafsīr* from Sulamī's *Ḥaqā'iq al-tafsīr* relating to the Qur'ān's first verse— some nine pages in the Beirut edition—Shiblī is quoted as having once repeated the divine name. On being questioned why he did not use the *shahāda* formula ("There is no god but God"), he replies in characteristic fashion: "I do not negate what is contrary [to Him]."[3] This familiar response shows his unwillingness to use the customary negating formula because other-than-God (what is negated) has, for him, no real existence or meaning.

Familiar ideas of Shiblī are also shown in his comment on Qur'ān 2:165: "believers have greater love for God," where he is quoted as saying that those who claim love for God but forget his remembrance for a moment are mockers and liars, and He treats them as such.[4]

Shiblī sometimes combines anagogical interpretation with a play on keywords from the Qur'ānic text, illustrating the process outlined by Böwering quoted above. Thus commenting on Qur'ān 3:97: "[Mecca] is the place [*maqām*] where Abraham stood," he states that the *maqām* ("place" but also "spiritual station") of Abraham is sincere friendship (*khulla*, cognate with *khalīl*, an epithet of Abraham), so one who sees there (on pilgrimage) the *maqām* of Abraham, the friend of God (*al-khalīl*), is honored, but one who sees there the *maqām* of the Real is more honored.[5]

On the same verse (Qur'ān 3:97): "Pilgrimage to the House is a duty," Sulamī makes a rare and brief editorial comment that there are symbolic meanings (*ishārāt*) to the pilgrimage. He relates that Shiblī once questioned a man who had just returned from the *ḥajj*, asking him about each action and stage of the prescribed duties, and whether he performed "spiritual" or anagogic actions in his pilgrimage. The man answers "no" to each question, though he performed the outward acts correctly. Shiblī tells him to return and perform the anagogical acts.[6]

An example of esoteric interpretation is that on Qur'ān 11:90: "Ask forgiveness from your Lord, and turn to Him in repentance: my Lord is merciful and most loving." Shiblī comments: "There is not one letter of all the letters [of the alphabet] which does not praise God Most High with its tongue, and it remembers Him in language which each of the letters has in its tongue: to each letter there is a tongue. This is a mystery of God Most High concerning His creation which is apprehended with increase of understanding and remembrance of Him."[7] In fact, this comment seems only remotely related to this verse. There are lacunae dots in the text following the previous comment, and since there are another thirty or so verses in this *sūra* omitted in the commentary, Shiblī's remarks may well relate to one of those.

A clear anagogic interpretation is offered at Qur'ān 13:17: "He sends water from the sky that fills riverbeds to overflowing, each according to its measure." Shiblī comments: "Hearts bear increases according to the measure of what the Real reveals to them of different sorts of bounties."[8]

A similar example of anagogic interpretation, though still retaining some sense of context, is at Qur'ān 20:12: "Moses! I am your Lord. Take off your shoes: you are in the sacred valley of Tuwa." Shiblī comments: "Take off all from yourself so you may reach Us with all; thus you may be, yet not be; thus you may be certain in the essence of unitive experience that your message is from Us, and your action is Our action."[9]

Reflecting Shiblī's sensitivity over his use of the first-person pronoun is the following comment on Qur᾿ān 38:76: "Iblis said, 'I am better than him [Adam]: You made me from fire, and him from clay.' " He comments: Iblis was worshipping for eternities without end, but he said once in his converse 'I,' so He cast him down. How then can 'I' also say 'Shiblī, Shiblī'? [10] Gerhard Böwering writes, "The final truth of Islamic mysticism—that there is only One Who can truly say, 'I'—is expressed in the ecstatic utterances of the Ṣūfīs, such as 'I am He' or 'I am the Real' (*anā l-ḥaqq*), secured in the innermost reaches of the soul through insight into the allegorical and anagogical meaning of the Qur᾿ān."[11]

In what could perhaps be termed a quasi-philological comment, Shiblī glosses two words for "knowledge" at Qur᾿ān 39:9: "How can those who know [*ya῾lamūna*] be equal to those who do not know?" Shiblī comments that acquired knowledge [*῾ilm*] is synonymous with *khubr*, while *khubr* is discovered or experienced [*mawjūd*] knowledge.[12]

Finally, an example where Shiblī uses word play, repeating words derived from the same root, at Qur᾿ān 53:23: "such people merely follow guesswork and the whims of their souls." Shiblī comments: For one who finds truth (*taḥaqqaqa*) in the reality (*ḥaqīqa*) of the Real (*al-ḥaqq*), then that is the soul of Reality (*al-ḥaqīqa*), for God says: "such people merely follow guesswork. . . ." [13]

These examples are certainly not exhaustive, but they illustrate the type of Qur᾿ānic exegesis attributed to Shiblī. Some of his comments have prima facie authenticity, as they clearly express views that he expounds elsewhere. Other comments are perhaps less securely based and could have come from many Sufi exegetes with similar ideas. One or two examples not included above are attributed to him but are almost certainly not authentic on stylistic grounds, being wordy and prolix, and thus probably authored by someone else.

CHAPTER 22

Conclusion

As our study of Shiblī draws to a close, we may conclude by summing up what we can know about this extraordinary saintly man.

Richard Gramlich, in his discussion of Shiblī, argues convincingly that a strictly historical life story eludes us, but the many faithfully transmitted sayings and anecdotes allow us to approach his figure.[1] Gramlich writes that it is not the historical biography that is preserved, but the spirituality and the nature of Shiblī's intellectual world. The central personality revealed has a claim to truth, though the narratives may or may not be historically based. Most of these narratives may be accepted as "true" in this sense, since the more fantastic stories don't fit the picture generally portrayed.[2]

Even if we cannot ascertain the real facts of Shiblī's life, his legacy is nevertheless very real and substantial. His piety, his integrity, and his single-mindedness, to name just a few of his virtues, have come down to us thanks to the various hagiographical sources available. Whether descriptions of events in his life are accurate or realistic is, in the end, not important for these sources. The ultimate purpose of the authors of these works is not to record facts, or even to throw light on Shiblī's character, but to conform to a paradigm of Sufi virtue and saintly conduct. Consciously or unconsciously, the source writers tell the life and death of Shiblī and the other Sufi masters in the way they want them to be understood. Ahmet Karamustafa writes that the material conveyed in these writings "was compiled and packaged in various ways to serve different but related functions: pedagogical guidance of aspirants, pious commemoration of past masters, building corporate solidarity among Sufis, and confident self-presentation and self-assertion vis-à-vis other groups competing for authority."[3]

If the details of his life events are sketchy and open to question, the configuration of his spiritual character is consistent across the sources. We know that his personality was complex—erratic, emotional, given to abrupt transitions—yet he was always open to the transcendent, to the possibilities and vicissitudes of divine grace acting on his life. Just as in Qur'ānic exegesis the "issue was not whether the Qur'ān was polysemous but rather how to express and limit the polysemy,"[4] so in Shiblī's life, his conundrum was not his enthusiasm for God, but how to express and limit that enthusiasm so that it did not destroy him. His spiritual restlessness, his desire for extreme renunciation, and his borderline sanity were constants in his struggle to integrate life in this world with otherworldly aspirations.

Shiblī's eccentricities can best be understood as intense expressions of his singular desire to experience transcendence. Those actions of his that cross the "line" of sanity are overflowings of this desire, intense moments (*awqāt*) when he is overwhelmed. This is still the case even if we acknowledge that his insanity and consequent hospitalizations are somewhat exaggerated by the later, mostly Persian, sources. His intensity is also a function of his deep and austere adherence to the absolute Oneness of the Real, a radical overzealousness that may be seen as insanity. His life can also be interpreted as an attempt to live and embody the Qur'ān profoundly, as Louis Massignon suggests,[5] in a way God's Word made flesh, though not in the Christian sense.

Massignon also asserts, on more questionable grounds, that "the union with God that he [Shiblī] passionately sought by the most bizarre means, is for him only an instantaneous shock, a contact impossible to maintain, a throbbing jealousy; he does not accept the notion of a *shahid* (= a permanent witness of God), which had gotten Hallaj accused of *hulul* [indwelling of the divine]." In contrast to Ḥallāj's "permanent state of inspiration," Massignon argues that "Shibli, each time his nature is disrupted, feels a divine presence moving through the disruption; his union with God is essentially atomistic, discontinuous."[6] Given what we can know of Shiblī through the earliest sources, it would seem more accurate to suppose that he experienced intervals of inspiration and intimacy with God that were longer lasting than the disjointed moments proposed by Massignon. Many of the anecdotes found in the *Kitāb al-lumaʿ*, and Sarrāj's lengthy exposition and interpretation of these,[7] suggest extended periods of what may be termed as psychologically altered state experiences. It may be supposed also that his periods of "insanity" were lengthier than Massignon suggests. These experiences are, arguably, part of his search for transcendence. It is true, however, that Shiblī was constantly and earnestly seeking that inspiration, always searching for the connection to the other world, the *waqt* (moment of inspiration) that would give direct access to the transcendent reality.

As for the alleged insanity that has clouded many people's perception of Shiblī, it was mentioned above that his intensity and overzealousness may be seen as a type of insane behavior. The sources also record many instances of his eccentricities of action or speech, yet these can be seen as symbolic and quasi-ritual actions, his acting out of his beliefs and his expression of his vision, rather than illustrating his madness. There are, however, the narratives about his committal to the insane asylum in Baghdad. It is easy to label a person as "mad" because of eccentric speech or behavior, and it is likely that this occurred in premodern Islamic society as much as it does today. It is much more difficult to understand the basis of such people's difference, and why they diverge from common behavior. In Shiblī's case, this was surely his intense pursuit of the divine presence and his attempt to experience transcendence no matter what the consequences. The characterization of Émile Dermenghem is that he expressed a certain *"folie"* in symbolic actions and words, capable of a playful yet at the same time deeply earnest acting out and realization of his faith.

The key to understanding his difference, however, is the way he perceived himself, not how others saw and labeled him. This key is expressed in Hujwīrī's *Kashf al-maḥjūb* in the revealing anecdote mentioned in chapter 19, that once when he was accosted by people calling him *majnūn* (insane), he replied: "You think I am mad, and I think you are sensible: may God increase my madness and your sense!" Hujwīrī adds: "inasmuch as my madness is the result of intense love of God, while your sense is the result of great heedlessness, may God increase my madness in order that I may become nearer to Him. . . ."[8] The implication of Hujwīrī's comment is clear: Shiblī's "insanity" allowed intimacy and greater love of God, and was thus welcomed.

Abū Nuʿaym records an anecdote about his behavior in the asylum, where Shiblī maintains that there is an equilibrium between his "drunken" and "sober" states. His declaration allows us to presume a harmony and continuum in his personality, not the disruption and imbalance of real insanity.

Richard Gramlich remarks perceptively that when the spiritual picture of Shiblī differs from the real Shiblī of history, it is like an artistic portrait differing from the portrayed person. He is then stylized and idealized with sharp features, typically exaggerated, and complemented or completed from the imagination.[9] It is my hope that this short study has shone some light on the true spiritual portrait of this remarkable man, and that some of the distortions and obscurities have been removed to reveal a fuller and brighter picture.

Notes

CHAPTER 1: INTRODUCTION

1. Richard Gramlich, *Alte Vorbilder des Sufitums: Erster Teil: Scheiche des Westens* (Wiesbaden: Harrassowitz Verlag, 1995), 513.
2. Ibid., 515.
3. Ibid., 518.
4. R. Stephen Humphreys, *Islamic History: A Framework for Inquiry*, rev. ed. (Princeton, N.J.: Princeton University Press, 1991), 194.

CHAPTER 2: THE HISTORICAL CONTEXT

1. Ira M. Lapidus, *A History of Islamic Societies*, 2nd ed. (Cambridge, U.K.: Cambridge University Press, 2002), 104.
2. Abū ʿAbd al-Raḥmān al-Sulamī, *Ṭabaqāt al-Ṣūfīya*, ed. Nūr al-Dīn Sharība, 2nd ed. (Cairo: Maktaba ʾl-Khānjī, 1969), 337.
3. Florian Sobieroj, "al-SHIBLĪ," in *Encyclopaedia of Islam*, new ed. vol. IX (Leiden: E. J. Brill, 1960–2002), 432.
4. John Renard, *Friends of God: Islamic Images of Piety, Commitment and Servanthood* (Berkeley: University of California Press, 2008), 68.
5. See Gramlich, *Alte Vorbilder*, 519–520 for details.
6. ʿAlī Ibn ʿUthmān al-Jullābī al-Hujwīrī, *Kashf al-maḥjūb*, ed. V. Zhukovski, trans. R. A. Nicholson (Tehran: Amīr Kabīr, 1336 a.h.s.), 182; (Lahore: Islamic Book Foundation, [1911]1982), 144.
7. Lapidus, *A History of Islamic Societies*, 106–108.
8. ʿAbdallāh Ibn Muḥammad al-Anṣārī, *Ṭabaqāt al-ṣūfīya*, ed. ʿAbd al-Ḥay Ḥabībī Qandahārī, 2nd ed. (Tehran: Kitāb-khāna Millī Irān, 1379 a.h.s.), 447.
9. Abū Nuʿaym al-Isfahānī, *Ḥilyat al-awliyāʾ wa-ṭabaqāt al-aṣfiyāʾ*, ed. Muṣṭafā ʿAbd al-Qādir ʿAṭā, vol. X (Beirut: Dār al-Kutub al-ʿIlmīya, 1988), 370.

CHAPTER 3: SARRĀJ'S *BOOK OF ILLUMINATIONS*

1. Alexander Knysh, *Islamic Mysticism: A Short History* (Leiden: Brill, 2000), 118.

2. Ibid., 119.

3. Ibid., 120.

4. Ahmet T. Karamustafa, *Sufism: The Formative Period* (Edinburgh: Edinburgh University Press, 2007), 67.

5. Ibid., 68–69.

6. Abū Naṣr ʿAbdallah b. ʿAlī al-Sarrāj al-Ṭūsī, *The Kitāb al-Lumaʿ fi ʾl-Taṣawwuf*, ed. R. A. Nicholson (London: Luzac and Co., [1963]1914), 36.

7. Robert K. C. Forman, *Mysticism, Mind, Consciousness* (Albany: State University of New York Press, 1999), 125.

8. Sarrāj, *Lumaʿ*, 36.

9. Ibid., 216, and variant version 354. See also John Renard, trans., *Knowledge of God in Classical Sufism: Foundations of Islamic Mystical Theology* (Mahwah: Paulist Press, 2004), 31.

10. Sarrāj, *Lumaʿ*, 223.

11. Forman, *Mysticism, Mind, Consciousness*, 105.

12. Sarrāj, *Lumaʿ*, 30.

13. Ibid., 34.

14. Ibid., 348.

15. Forman, *Mysticism, Mind, Consciousness*, 125.

16. Ibid., 11–13.

17. Sarrāj, *Lumaʿ*, 46.

18. Ibid., 47; translation in Michael A. Sells, *Early Islamic Mysticism: Sufi, Qurʾan, Miʿraj, Poetic and Theological Writings* (Mahwah: Paulist Press, 1996), 203.

19. Farīd al-Dīn ʿAṭṭār, *Tadhkirat al-awliyāʾ*, ed. Muḥammad Esteʿlāmī (Tehran: Zawwār, 1346 a.h.s.), 555; ed. R. A. Nicholson, London: Luzac and Co., Leiden: E. J. Brill, 1905–1907, vol. 2, 180.

20. Sarrāj, *Lumaʿ*, 183–184, and slightly varied, 400.

21. Ibid., 206.

22. *Ibn Khallikan's Biographical Dictionary*, vol. 1, trans. Bn Mac Guckin de Slane (Beirut: Librairie du Liban, 1970 repr.), 511.

23. ʿAṭṭār, *Tadhkirat*, ed. Esteʿlāmī, 540; ed. Nicholson, vol. 2, 164.

24. Sarrāj, *Lumaʿ*, 50.

25. Ibid., 49–50; Sells, *Early Islamic Mysticism*, 206.

26. Sarrāj, *Lumaʿ*, 52; Sells, *Early Islamic Mysticism*, 209.

27. Sarrāj, *Lumaʿ*, 307.

28. Ibid., 282–283.

29. Ibid., 292.

30. Ibid., 304.

31. Reading *fa-innanī* with Nicholson's manuscript A, and as in the German translation of Richard Gramlich, *Schlaglichter über das Sufitum: Abū Nasr as-Sarrāǧs Kitāb al-lumaʿ eingeleitet, übersetzt und kommentiert* (Stuttgart: Franz Steiner Verlag, 1990), 493.

32. Sarrāj, *Lumaʿ*, 355–356.

33. Ibid., 206.

34. Ibid., 233–234.

35. Ibid., 405.

36. Forman, *Mysticism, Mind, Consciousness*, 164.

37. Sarrāj, *Lumaʿ*, 405. For a fuller account of ecstasy and mystical experience see Carl W. Ernst, *Words of Ecstasy in Sufism* (Albany: State University of New York Press, 1985), and my *A Psychology of Early Sufi samāʿ: Listening and Altered States* (Abingdon, U.K. and New York: RoutledgeCurzon), 2004.

38. Sarrāj, *Lumaʿ*, 91.

39. Abū ʿAbd al-Raḥmān al-Sulamī, *Ḥaqāʾiq al-tafsīr*, vol. 2, ed. Sayyid ʿImrān (Beirut: Dār al-Kutub al-ʿIlmīya, 2001), 43.

40. Sarrāj, *Lumaʿ*, 91.

41. Ibid., 298.

42, Sulamī, *Ḥaqāʾiq al-tafsīr*, vol. 1, 101.

43. Sarrāj, *Lumaʿ*, 400–402.

44. Ibid., 402.

45. Ibid., 194.

46. Ibid., 360.

47. Ibid., 360–361.

48. Ibid., 395–396.

49. Ibid., 396.

50. Ibid., 397.

51. Ibid., 402.

52. Ibid., 402–403.

53. Ibid., 405.

54. Ibid., 405–406

55. Ibid., 406.

56. Ibid., 104, 210.

57. Ibid., 210.

58. Ibid., 209.

59. Ibid., 406.

CHAPTER 4: KALĀBĀDHĪ'S *BOOK OF UNDERSTANDING*

1. Knysh, *Islamic Mysticism: A Short History*, 123.

2. Ibid., 124.

3. Karamustafa, *Sufism: The Formative Period*, 69–71.

4. Abū Bakr Muḥammad Ibn Isḥāq al-Kalābādhī, *al-Taʿarruf li-madhhab ahl al-taṣawwuf*, ed. ʿAbd al-Ḥalīm Maḥmūd (Cairo: Maktaba al-Thaqāfa al-Ḥīnīya, n.d.), 30–32; trans. A. J. Arberry, *The Doctrine of the Sūfīs* (Lahore: Sh. Muhammad Ashraf, 1966 repr.), 14.

5. Kalābādhī, *Taʿarruf*, 94; Arberry, 93.

6. Kalābādhī, *Taʿarruf*, 106; Arberry, 109.

7. Kalābādhī, *Taʿarruf*, 135; Arberry, 150.

8. Forman, *Mysticism, Mind, Consciousness*, 145.

9. Kalābādhī, *Taʿarruf*, 145; Arberry, 161.

10. ʿAṭṭār, *Tadhkirat*, ed. Esteʿlāmī, 542; ed. Nicholson, vol. 2, 166.

CHAPTER 5: SULAMĪ'S *GENERATIONS OF THE SUFIS*

1. See further, Gerhard Böwering's article, "al-SULAMĪ," in *Encyclopaedia of Islam*, new ed., vol. IX (Leiden: E. J. Brill, 1960–2002), 811–812.

2. See further, Jawid A. Mojaddedi, *The Biographical Tradition in Sufism: The* tabaqāt *Genre from al-Sulamī to Jāmī* (Richmond, U.K.: Curzon Press, 2001).

3. Renard, *Friends of God*, 6.

4. Karamustafa, *Sufism: The Formative Period*, 63.

5. Mojaddedi, *The Biographical Tradition in Sufism*, 15.

6. Knysh, *Islamic Mysticism: A Short History*, 127.

7. Gerhard Böwering, "The Qurʾān Commentary of al-Sulamī," in *Islamic Studies Presented to Charles J. Adams*, ed. W. B. Hallaq and D. P. Little (Leiden: E. J. Brill, 1991), 50.

8. Ibid., 56.

9. Ibid.

10. See further, Alexander Knysh, "Sūfism and the Qurʾān," in *Encyclopaedia of the Qurʾān*, vol. V (Leiden: E. J. Brill, 2001–2006), 139.

11. Abū ʿAbd al-Raḥmān al-Sulamī, *Kitāb Ṭabaqāt al-Ṣūfiyya*, ed. Johannes Pedersen (Leiden: E. J. Brill, 1960), 23.

12. Ibid., 26ff.

13. Ibid., 26, 28–29.

14, Ibid., 29–30.

15. Ibid., 35.

16. Ibid., 35–36.

17. Ibid., 50–57.

18. Sulamī, *Ṭabaqāt al-Ṣūfiya*, ed. Sharība, 337.

19. Ibid.

20. Ibid., 341; ed. Pedersen, 343.

21. *Ṭabaqāt*, ed. Sharība, 343; ed. Pedersen, 346.

22. *Ṭabaqāt*, ed. Sharība, 343; ed. Pedersen, 347.
23. *Ṭabaqāt*, ed. Sharība, 340; ed. Pedersen, 342.
24. *Ṭabaqāt*, ed. Sharība, 341; ed. Pedersen, 343.
25. Ibid.
26. *Ṭabaqāt*, ed. Sharība, 347; ed. Pedersen, 352.
27. *Ṭabaqāt*, ed. Sharība, 342; ed. Pedersen, 345.
28. *Ṭabaqāt*, ed. Sharība, 344. Not in Pedersen's edition.
29. *Ṭabaqāt*, ed. Sharība, 345. Not in Pedersen's edition.
30. *Ṭabaqāt*, ed. Sharība, 345; ed. Pedersen, 353–354.
31. Forman, *Mysticism, Mind, Consciousness*, 137–138.
32. Reading with Pedersen's edition; Sharība has "proved."
33. *Ṭabaqāt*, ed. Sharība, 342; ed. Pedersen, 344–345.
34. Pedersen has "what is not hidden."
35. *Ṭabaqāt*, ed. Sharība, 347; ed. Pedersen, 351.
36. Mojaddedi, *The Biographical Tradition in Sufism*, 37.
37. Ibid., 37–38.

CHAPTER 6: ABŪ NUʿAYM'S *ORNAMENT OF GOD'S FRIENDS*

1. See further, W. Madelung's article, "ABŪ NOʿAYM al-ESFAHĀNĪ," in *Encyclopaedia Iranica*, vol. 1 (London: Routledge and Kegan Paul, 1985, 354–355; and J. Pedersen's article "ABŪ NUʿAYM al-ISFAHĀNĪ," in *Encyclopaedia of Islam*, new ed., vol. 1 (Leiden: E. J. Brill, 1960–2002), 142–143.

2. Raif G. Khoury, "Importance et authenticité des texts de *Ḥilyat al-awliyāʾ wa-ṭabaqat al-aṣfiyāʾ* d'Abū Nuʿaym al-Isbahānī," in *Studia Islamica* 46 (1977): 83. See further, Mojaddedi, *The Biographical Tradition in Sufism*, 42ff.

3. Knysh, *Islamic Mysticism: A Short History*, 129.

4. Mojaddedi, *The Biographical Tradition in Sufism*, 64; Karamustafa, *Sufism: The Formative Period*, 89.

5. Karamustafa, *Sufism: The Formative Period*, 90.

6. Abū Nuʿaym, *Ḥilyat al-awliyāʾ*, vol. X, 367.

7. Ibid., 368.

8. ʿAṭṭār, *Tadhkirat*, ed. Esteʿlāmī, 538; ed. Nicholson, vol. 2, 163.

9. Sarrāj, *Lumaʿ*, 350; Abū Nuʿaym, *Ḥilyat al-awliyāʾ*, vol. X, 369.

10. Sulamī, *Ṭabaqāt*, ed. Sharība, 341; Abū Nuʿaym, *Ḥilyat al-awliyāʾ*, vol. X, 370.

11. Abū Nuʿaym, *Ḥilyat al-awliyāʾ*, vol. X, 372.

12. Sarrāj, *Lumaʿ*, 104, 210; Abū Nuʿaym, *Ḥilyat al-awliyāʾ*, vol. X, 371.

13. Abū Nuʿaym, *Ḥilyat al-awliyāʾ*, vol. X, 368.

14. Mojaddedi, *The Biographical Tradition in Sufism*, 56.

CHAPTER 7: QUSHAYRĪ'S *TREATISE*

1. See further, H. Halm's article "al-ḲUSHAYRĪ," in *Encyclopaedia of Islam*, new ed., vol. V (Leiden: E. J. Brill, 1960–2002), 526–527.

2. Karamustafa, *Sufism: The Formative Period*, 97.

3. Ibid., 99.

4. Knysh, *Islamic Mysticism: A Short History*, 132.

5. See further, Mojaddedi, *The Biographical Tradition in Sufism*, 100–101.

6. ʿAbd al-Karīm al-Qushayrī, *al-Risālat al-Qushayrīya fī ʿilm al-taṣawwuf*, ed. Maʿruf Zarīq and ʿAlī Balṭajī (Beirut: Dār al-Jīl, n.d.), 419–420.

7. See E. W. Lane, *An Arabic-English Lexicon*, vol. 2 (Cambridge, U.K.: Islamic Texts Society Trust, 1984), 1910.

8. Qushayrī, *Risāla*, 420.

9. Ibid., 221–222; trans. B. R. von Schlegell, *Principles of Sufism* (Oneonta: Mizan Press, 1990), 207.

10. Qushayrī, *Risāla*, 60; Cf. trans. Sells, *Early Islamic Mysticism*, 109.

11. Qushayrī, *Risāla*, 302.

12. Ibid., 41.

13. Ibid., 312; Cf. Von Schlegell, *Principles of Sufism*, 318.

14. See further, Florian Sobieroj, "Love in the Mystical Discourse and Experience of Abū Bakr Shiblī," in *Sufi*, 23, 1994, 10–15.

15. Qushayrī, *Risāla*, 321; Cf. Von Schlegell, *Principles of Sufism*, 330.

16. Sarrāj, *Lumaʿ*, 111.

17. Hujwīrī, *Kashf*, 394; trans. Nicholson, 305.

18. ʿAṭṭār, *Tadhkirat*, ed. Esteʿlāmī, 419; ed. Nicholson, vol. 2, 61. Cf. Gramlich, *Schlaglichter*, 187.

19. Qushayrī, *Risāla*, 322; Von Schlegell, *Principles of Sufism*, 331.

20. Qushayrī, *Risāla*, 324; Cf. Von Schlegell, *Principles of Sufism*, 334.

21. See my *A Psychology of Early Sufi samāʿ*.

22. Sarrāj, *Lumaʿ*, 272.

23. Qushayrī, *Risāla*, 340–341.

24. Ibid., 344; Sarrāj, *Lumaʿ*, 281–282; words in italics are not in *Risāla* text.

25. Some manuscripts of Sarrāj's *Lumaʿ* other than Nicholson's printed text have the same reading as Qushayrī's, however. Cf. Gramlich, *Schlaglichter*, 409.

26. Sarrāj, *Lumaʿ*, 282–283; see chapter 3.

27. Qushayrī, *Risāla*, 344–345.

28. See further, my *A Psychology of Early Sufi samāʿ*, especially 167.

29. Martin Lings, *Sufi Poems: A Mediaeval Anthology* (Cambridge, U.K.: Islamic Texts Society, 2004), 41.

30. Qushayrī, *Risāla*, 349.

31. See my *A Psychology of Early Sufi samāʿ*, 169–170.
32. Sarrāj, *Lumaʿ*, 50; see chapter 3.
33. See further Gramlich, *Schlaglichter*, 97.
34. Abū Nuʿaym, *Ḥilyat al-awliyāʾ*, vol. X, 372.
35. Qushayrī, *Risāla*, 306.
36. ʿAṭṭār, *Tadhkirat*, ed. Esteʿlāmī, 556; ed. Nicholson, vol. 2, 181.
37. See further, Jawid A. Mojaddedi, "Legitimizing Sufism in al-Qushayri's *Risala*," in *Studia Islamica* 90 (2000): 37–50.

CHAPTER 8: HUJWĪRĪ'S *REVEALING THE VEILED*

1. See the introduction in Nicholson's translation of Hujwīrī's *Kashf*; Hidayet Hosain [and H. Massé] article "HUDJWĪRĪ," in *Encyclopaedia of Islam*, new ed., vol. III (Leiden: E. J. Brill, 1960–2002), 546; Mojaddedi, *The Biographical Tradition in Sufism*, 125ff.
2. Hujwīrī, *Kashf*, 110; trans. Nicholson, 91.
3. Mojaddedi, *The Biographical Tradition in Sufism*, 126.
4. Hujwīrī, trans. Nicholson, xxiii.
5. Karamustafa, *Sufism: The Formative Period*, 102–103.
6. Hujwīrī, *Kashf*, 465; trans. Nicholson, 356.
7. Hujwīrī, *Kashf*, 195–197; trans. Nicholson, 155–156.
8. Hujwīrī, *Kashf*, 196; trans. Nicholson, 156.
9. Sarrāj, *Lumaʿ*, 206.
10. Qushayrī, *Risāla*, 366.
11. Hujwīrī, *Kashf*, 460; trans. Nicholson, 353.
12. Sarrāj, *Lumaʿ*, 400–402.
13. Hujwīrī, *Kashf*, 287; trans. Nicholson, 228.
14. Hujwīrī, *Kashf*, 374ff; trans. Nicholson, 291ff.
15. Hujwīrī, *Kashf*, 377; trans. Nicholson, 293.
16. Hujwīrī, *Kashf*, 378; trans. Nicholson, 294.

CHAPTER 9: ANṢĀRĪ'S *GENERATIONS OF THE SUFIS*

1. See Serge de Laugier de Beaurecueil's article "ʿAbdallāh al-ANṢĀRĪ," in *Encyclopaedia Iranica*, vol. 1, 187–190; and idem, article "al-ANṢĀRĪ," in *Encyclopaedia of Islam*, new ed., vol. I (Leiden: E. J. Brill, 1960–2002), 515–516.
2. *Encyclopaedia Iranica*, vol. 1, 189.
3. Mojaddedi, *The Biographical Tradition in Sufism*, 70ff.
4. Karamustafa, *Sufism: The Formative Period*, 96.
5. Anṣārī, *Ṭabaqāt*, 377.
6. Ibid., 378.

7. Ibid., 379.

8. Ibid.

9. Mojaddedi, *The Biographical Tradition in Sufism*, 93–96.

CHAPTER 10: RŪZBIHĀN'S *EXPLANATION OF ECSTATIC SAYINGS*

1. For biographical details see Carl W. Ernst's article "RŪZBIHĀN," in *Encyclopaedia of Islam*, new ed., vol. VIII (Leiden: E. J. Brill, 1960–2002), 651–652.

2. See further Carl W. Ernst, *Rūzbihān Baqlī: Mysticism and the Rhetoric of Sainthood in Persian Sufism* (Richmond, U.K.: Curzon Press, 1996).

3. *Encyclopaedia of Islam*, new ed., vol. VIII (Leiden: E. J. Brill, 1960–2002), 651.

4. Rūzbihān Baqlī, *Commentaire sur les paradoxes des Soufis (Sharḥ-e shaṭḥīyāt)*, ed. Henry Corbin (Tehran: Institute Français d'Iranologie de Téhéran, [1966]1981), 251.

5. Ibid., 259.

6. Ibid., 261.

7. Ibid., 264.

8. Ibid., 265.

9. Ibid., 267.

CHAPTER 11: ʿAṬṬĀR'S *MEMOIRS OF GOD'S FRIENDS*

1. ʿAṭṭār, Farīd al-Dīn, *Muslim Saints and Mystics: Episodes from the Tadhkirat al-Auliyaʾ*, trans. A. J. Arberry (London: Routledge and Kegan Paul [1966]1979), 17.

2. ʿAṭṭār, *Tadhkirat*, ed. Esteʿlāmī, xxxvi–xxxvii.

3. ʿAṭṭār, *Tadhkirat*, ed. Nicholson, vol. 2, English part, 4.

4. Shahram Pazouki, "Sufi Saints and Sainthood in *ʿAṭṭār's Tadhkirat al-awliyāʾ*," in Leonard Lewisohn and Christopher Shackle (eds.), *ʿAṭṭār and the Persian Sufi Tradition: The Art of Spiritual Flight* (London, New York: I. B. Tauris and the Institute of Ismaili Studies, 2006), 64.

5. Paul Losensky, "Words and Deeds: Message and Structure in *ʿAṭṭār's Tadhkirat al-awliyāʾ*," in Lewisohn and Shackle, *ʿAṭṭār and the Persian Sufi Tradition*, 76.

6. ʿAṭṭār, *Muslim Saints and Mystics*, trans. Arberry, 11–12.

7. Ibid., 13–14.

8. ʿAṭṭār, *Tadhkirat*, ed. Esteʿlāmī, 345–346; ed. Nicholson, vol. 1, 328–329; trans. Arberry, 197–198.

9. ʿAṭṭār, *Tadhkirat*, ed. Esteʿlāmī, 370; ed. Nicholson, vol. 2, 12.

10. ʿAṭṭār, *Tadhkirat*, ed. Esteʿlāmī, 372; ed. Nicholson, vol. 2, 14; adapted from Qushayrī, *Risāla*, 195; Von Schlegell, *Principles of Sufism*, 166.

11. ʿAṭṭār, *Tadhkirat*, ed. Esteʿlāmī, 373; ed. Nicholson, vol. 2, 15–16; trans. Arberry, 206.

12. ʿAṭṭār, *Tadhkirat*, ed. Esteʿlāmī, 393; ed. Nicholson, vol. 2, 36.

13. Sarrāj, *Lumaʿ*, 233.

14. ʿAṭṭār, *Tadhkirat*, ed. Esteʿlāmī, 396; ed. Nicholson, vol. 2, 38–39; trans. Arberry, 216–217.

15. ʿAṭṭār, *Tadhkirat*, ed. Esteʿlāmī, 406–407; ed. Nicholson, vol. 2, 48–49; trans. Arberry, 223–225.

16. Abū Nuʿaym, *Ḥilyat al-awliyāʾ*, vol. X, 250–251.

17. A. J. Arberry, *Pages from the Kitāb al-Lumaʿ of Abū Naṣr al-Sarrāj* (London: Luzac and Co., 1947), 5–6.

18. Karamustafa, *Sufism: The Formative Period*, 12; see Ernst's discussion of these trials in *Words of Ecstasy in Sufism*, 97ff.

19. F. Steingass, *Persian-English Dictionary* (London: Routledge and Kegan Paul [1892] 1977), 932. ʿAṭṭar, *Tadhkirat*, ed. Esteʿlāmī, 408–409; ed. Nicholson, vol. 2, 50–51; trans. Arberry, 227.

20. ʿAṭṭār, *Tadhkirat*, ed. Esteʿlāmī, 410; ed. Nicholson, vol. 2, 52; trans. Arberry, 228.

21. ʿAṭṭār, *Tadhkirat*, ed. Esteʿlāmī, 438; ed. Nicholson, vol. 2, 77.

22. Hujwīrī, *Kashf*, 190; trans. Nicholson, 151.

23. ʿAṭṭār, *Tadhkirat*, ed. Esteʿlāmī, 510; ed. Nicholson, vol. 2, 136.

24. Ibid.

25. ʿAṭṭār, *Tadhkirat*, ed. Esteʿlāmī, 517; ed. Nicholson, vol. 2, 143; trans. Arberry, 269.

26. ʿAṭṭār, *Tadhkirat*, ed. Esteʿlāmī, 519; ed. Nicholson, vol. 2, 145.

CHAPTER 12: JĀMĪ'S *BREATHS OF INTIMACY*

1. Cl. Huart [and H. Massé], article "DJĀMĪ," in *Encyclopaedia of Islam*, new ed., vol. II (Leiden: E. J. Brill, 1960–2002), 422.

2. Mojaddedi, *The Biographical Tradition in Sufism*, 152.

3. Ibid., 153.

4. *Encyclopaedia of Islam*, new ed., vol. II (Leiden: E. J. Brill, 1960–2002), 422.

5. Mojaddedi, *The Biographical Tradition in Sufism*, 153.

6. ʿAbd al-Raḥmān Ibn Aḥmad Jāmī, *Nafaḥāt al-uns min ḥaḍarāt al-quds*, ed. Mahdī Tawḥīdī Pūr (Tehran: Intishārāt ʿIlmī, 1375 a.h.s.), 180.

7. Ibid., 182–183.

8. Ibid., 183.

9. A. J. Arberry, *Classical Persian Literature* (London: George Allen and Unwin, 1958), 425ff.

CHAPTER 13: TWO NON-SUFI HISTORIANS: KHAṬĪB AL-BAGHDĀDĪ AND AL-DHAHABĪ

1. Abū Bakr Aḥmad Ibn ʿAlī al-Khaṭīb al-Baghdādī, *Taʾrīkh Baghdād*, vol. 14, ed. Muṣṭafā ʿAbd al-Qādir ʿAṭā (Beirut: Dār al-Kutub al-ʿIlmīya, 1997 repr.), 394–395.

2. Ibid., 396.

3. R. Sellheim's article, "al-KHAṬĪB al-BAGHDĀDĪ," in *Encyclopaedia of Islam*, new ed., vol. IV (Leiden: E. J. Brill, 1960–2002), 1111.

4. See further, Fedwa Malti-Douglas, "Controversy and Its Effects in the Biographical Tradition of al-Khaṭīb al-Baghdādī," in *Studia Islamica* 46 (1977):130–131.

5. *Ibn Khallikan's Biographical Dictionary*, vol. 1, 511ff.

6. Sulamī, *Ṭabaqāt al-Ṣūfīya*, ed. Pedersen, 54ff.

7. Moh. Ben Cheneb [and J. De Somogyi], "al-DHAHABĪ," in *Encyclopaedia of Islam*, new ed. vol. II (Leiden: E. J. Brill, 1960–2002), 215.

8. Ibid.

9. Shams al-Dīn al-Dhahabī, *Siyar aʿlām al-nubalāʾ*, vol. 15, ed. Shuʿayb al-Arnāʾūṭ and Ḥusayn al-Asad (Beirut: Muʾassasa al-Risāla, 1981–1988), 367.

10. Ibid., 368.

11. Ibid., 369.

CHAPTER 14: SHIBLĪ AND THE SOURCES: CONCLUSIONS

1. Mojaddedi, *The Biographical Tradition in Sufism*, 179.

2. Ibid., 180.

3. Ibid., 179.

4. Ibid., 180–181.

5. Ibid., 56.

6. Ibid., 55.

7. Chase F. Robinson, *Islamic Historiography* (Cambridge, U.K.: Cambridge University Press, 2003), 19.

8. Ibid., 37–38.

9. Karamustafa, *Sufism: The Formative Period*, 89; Mojaddedi, *The Biographical Tradition in Sufism*, 64.

10. Robinson, *Islamic Historiography*, 54.

11. Ibid., 62.

12. Ibid., 131.

13. Using Tarif Khalidi's expression in *Arabic Historical Thought in the Classical Period* (Cambridge, U.K.: Cambridge University Press, 1994), 32.

14. Robinson, *Islamic Historiography*, 63.

15. Alison Goddard Elliott, *Roads to Paradise: Reading the Lives of the Early Saints* (Hanover, N.H. and London: University Press of New England, 1987), 10–11).

16. Ibid., 180.

17. Eric L. Ormsby, "The Taste of Truth: The Structure of Experience in al-Ghazālī's *al-Munqidh min al-Ḍalāl*," in *Islamic Studies Presented to Charles J. Adams*, ed. W. B. Hallaq and D. P. Little (Leiden: E. J. Brill, 1991), 147.

CHAPTER 15: NARRATIVE STRUCTURES AND STYLES

1. Hugh Kennedy, *When Baghdad Ruled the Muslim World: The Rise and Fall of Islam's Greatest Dynasty* (Cambridge, Mass.: Da Capo Press, 2004), 12.

2. Ibid.

3. Karamustafa, *Sufism: The Formative Period*, 83–84.

4. Louis Massignon, *The Passion of al-Hallaj, Mystic and Martyr of Islam*, abridged edition, trans. and ed. Herbert Mason (Princeton, N.J.: Princeton University Press, 1994), xxii.

5. Karamustafa, *Sufism: The Formative Period*, 84.

6. Mojaddedi, *The Biographical Tradition in Sufism*, 34.

7. Karamustafa, *Sufism: The Formative Period*, 12.

8. Elliott, *Roads to Paradise*, 180.

CHAPTER 16: THE NATURE OF SHIBLĪ'S SAYINGS

1. Annemarie Schimmel, *Mystical Dimensions of Islam* (Chapel Hill: University of North Carolina Press, 1975), 16, quoting Hujwīrī, *Kashf*, trans. Nicholson, 38.

2. Schimmel, *Mystical Dimensions*, 79.

3. Sarrāj, *Lumaʿ*, 46.

4. Ibid.

5. Kalābādhī, *Taʿarruf*, 94; trans. Arberry, 93.

6. Sarrāj, *Lumaʿ*, 34.

7. Ibid., 52; trans. Sells, *Early Islamic Mysticism*, 209.

8. Sarrāj, *Lumaʿ*, 402.

9. Ernst, *Words of Ecstasy in Sufism*, 48.

10. Sarrāj, *Lumaʿ*, 282–283.

11. Ibid., 292.

12. Ibid., 304.

13. See also my *A Psychology of Early Sufi samāʿ*.

14. Sarrāj, *Lumaʿ*, 397.

15. Ibid., 395–406.
16. Ibid., 405.
17. Ibid., 405–406.
18. Ibid., 395–396.
19. Ernst, *Words of Ecstasy in Sufism*, 49.
20. Ibid., 39; idem., "SHAṬḤ," in *Encyclopaedia of Islam*, new ed., vol. IX (Leiden: E. J. Brill, 1960–2002), 362.
21. Ernst, *Words of Ecstasy in Sufism*, 51.

CHAPTER 17: SHIBLĪ AND JUNAYD

1. Christopher Melchert, "The Transition from Asceticism to Mysticism at the Middle of the Ninth Century C.E.," *Studia Islamica* 83 (1996): 66.
2. Ibid., 66–67.
3. Sarrāj, *Lumaʿ*, 307.
4. Ibid., 404.
5. Ibid.
6. Ibid., 233–234.
7. Gramlich, *Schlaglichter*, 355, and idem, *Alte Vorbilder*, 558–559.
8. Kalābādhī, *Taʿarruf*, 145; trans. Arberry, 161.
9. Abū Nuʿaym, *Ḥilyat al-awliyāʾ*, vol. X, 371.
10. Qushayrī, *Risāla*, 195; trans. Von Schlegell, *Principles of Sufism*, 166.
11. Anṣārī, *Ṭabaqāt*, 378; repeated by Jāmī in *Nafaḥāt al-uns*, 180.
12. Anṣārī, *Ṭabaqāt*, 379.
13. Ibid.

CHAPTER 18: SHIBLĪ AND HALLĀJ

1. Massignon, *Passion*, abridged ed., 46.
2. ʿAṭṭār, *Tadhkirat*, ed. Esteʿlāmī, 536; ed. Nicholson, vol. 2, 160–161.
3. Hujwīrī, *Kashf*, 190; trans. Nicholson, 151.
4. Gramlich, *Alte Vorbilder*, 560–561.
5. ʿAṭṭār, *Tadhkirat*, ed. Esteʿlāmī, 519; ed. Nicholson, vol. 2, 145.
6. ʿAṭṭār, *Tadhkirat*, ed. Esteʿlāmī, 517; ed. Nicholson, vol. 2, 143.
7. Massignon, *Passion*, abridged ed., 288–289.
8. See Massignon, *Passion* for details of these stories.
9. ʿAṭṭār, *Tadhkirat*, ed. Esteʿlāmī, 519; ed. Nicholson, vol. 2., 145.
10. Massignon, *Passion*, abridged ed., 47–48.

6. Ibid., 110–112.
7. Ibid., 325.
8. Böwering, *The Minor Qurʾān Commentary*, 67.
9. Sulamī, *Ḥaqāʾiq al-tafsīr*, vol. 1, 436.
10. Böwering, *The Minor Qurʾān Commentary*, 147–148.
11. Gerhard Böwering, "The Scriptural 'Senses' in Medieval Ṣūfī Qurʾān Exegesis," in J. D. McAuliffe, B. D.Walfish, and J. W.Goering (eds.), *With Reverence for the Word: Medieval Scriptural Exegesis in Judaism, Christianity and Islam* (New York: Oxford University Press, 2003), 357.
12. Sulamī, *Ḥaqāʾiq al-tafsīr*, vol. 2, 193.
13. Ibid., 286.

CHAPTER 22: CONCLUSION

1. Gramlich, *Alte Vorbilder*, 516.
2. Ibid., 518.
3. Karamustafa, *Sufism: The Formative Period*, 84.
4. Herbert Berg, "Polysemy in the Qurʾān," in *Encyclopaedia of the Qurʾān*, vol. IV (Leiden: Brill, 2001–2006), 155.
5. Massignon, *Passion*, abridged ed., 288.
6. Ibid., 45–46.
7. Sarrāj, *Lumaʿ*, 395–406.
8. Hujwīrī, *Kashf*, 196; trans. Nicholson, 156.
9. Gramlich, *Alte Vorbilder*, 518.

Bibliography

Afnan, S. M., *A Philosophical Lexicon in Persian and Arabic*. Beirut: Dar el-Machreq, 1969.

Aigle, Denise, "Les biographies de saints de ʿAṭṭâr et de Ğâmī, prolongements des écrits fondateurs du soufisme," *Anatolia Moderna: Yeni Anadolu* 5 (1994): 1–21.

al-Anṣārī, ʿAbdallāh Ibn Muḥammad, *Ṭabaqāt al-ṣūfīya*, ed. ʿAbd al-Ḥay Ḥabībī Qandahārī, 2nd ed. Tehran: Kitāb-khāna Millī Irān, 1379 a.h.s.

Arberry, A. J., *Classical Persian Literature*. London: George Allen and Unwin, 1958.

———, *Pages from the Kitāb al-Lumaʿ of Abū Naṣr al-Sarrāj*. London: Luzac and Co., 1947.

ʿAṭṭār, Farīd al-Dīn, *Muslim Saints and Mystics: Episodes from the Tadhkirat al-Auliyaʾ*, translated by A. J. Arberry. London: Routledge and Kegan Paul, 1966 (repr. 1979).

———, *Tadhkirat al-awliyāʾ*, ed. Muḥammad Esteʿlāmī. Tehran: Zawwār, 1346 a.h.s.

———, *Tadhkiratu ʾl-awliyāʾ*, ed. R. A. Nicholson, 2 vols. London: Luzac and Co, Leiden: E. J. Brill, 1905–1907.

Avery, Kenneth, *A Psychology of Early Sufi samāʿ: Listening and Altered States*. Abingdon, U.K. and New York: RoutledgeCurzon, 2004.

Baqlī, Rūzbihān, *Commentaire sur les paradoxes des Soufis (Sharḥ-e shaṭḥīyāt)*, ed. Henry Corbin. Tehran: Institute Français d'Iranologie de Téhéran, 1966 (1981 repr.)

Beaurecueil, Serge de Laugier de, "ʿAbdallāh al-ANṢĀRĪ," in *Encyclopaedia Iranica*, vol. I, London: Routledge and Kegan Paul, 1985–continuing, 187–190.

———, "al-ANṢĀRĪ," in *Encyclopaedia of Islam*, new ed., vol I, Leiden: E. J. Brill, 1960–2002, 515–516.

Berg, Herbert, "Polysemy in the Qurʾān," in *Encyclopaedia of the Qurʾān*, vol. IV, Leiden: Brill, 2001–2006, 155–158.

Böwering, Gerhard, "al-KALĀBĀDHĪ," in *The Encyclopedia of Religion*, vol. 8, New York: Macmillan, 1987, 230–231.

———, (ed.), *The Minor Qur'ān Commentary of Abū ʿAbd ar-Raḥmān Muḥammad b. Al-Ḥusayn as-Sulamī (d. 412/1021)*. 2nd ed. Beirut: Dar el-Machreq Sarl, 1997.

———, "The Qur'ān Commentary of al-Sulamī," in *Islamic Studies Presented to Charles J. Adams*, ed. Wael B. Hallaq and Donald P. Little. Leiden: E. J. Brill, 1991, 41–56.

———, "The Scriptural 'Senses' in Medieval Ṣūfī Qur'ān Exegesis," in *With Reverence for the Word: Medieval Scriptural Exegesis in Judaism, Christianity, and Islam* ed. J. D. McAuliffe, B. D.Walfish, and J. W. Goering, New York: Oxford University Press, 2003, 346–365.

———, "al-SULAMĪ," in *Encyclopaedia of Islam*, new ed., vol IX, Leiden: E. J. Brill, 1960–2002, 811–812.

Bruijn, J. T. P. de, "The *Qalandariyyāt* in Persian Mystical Poetry, from Sanā'ī Onwards," in *The Legacy of Mediaeval Persian Sufism*, ed. Leonard Lewisohn. London: Khaniqahi Nimatullahi, 1992, 75–86.

The Cambridge History of Arabic Literature: ʿAbbasid belles-lettres, ed. J. Ashtiany, T. M. Johnstone, J. D. Latham, R. B. Serjeant, and G. R. Smith. Cambridge, U.K.: Cambridge University Press, 1990.

The Cambridge History of Arabic Literature: Religion, Learning and Science in the ʿAbbasid Period, ed. M. J. L. Young, J. D. Latham, and R. B. Serjeant, Cambridge, U.K.: Cambridge University Press, 1990.

Chabbi, Jacqueline, "Réflections sur le soufisme iranien primitif," in *Journal Asiatique* 266 (1978): 37–55.

Cheneb, Moh. Ben [and J. De Somogyi], "al-DHAHABĪ," in *Encyclopaedia of Islam*, new ed., vol. II, Leiden: E. J. Brill, 1960–2002, 214–216.

Cooperson, Michael, *Classical Arabic Biography: The Heirs of the Prophets in the Age of al-Ma'mūn*. Cambridge, U.K.: Cambridge University Press, 2000.

Dermenghem, Émile, *Vies des saints musulmans*. Arles: Actes Sud, 2005, repr.

al-Dhahabī, Shams al-Dīn, *Siyar aʿlām al-nubalā'*, ed. Shuʿayb al-Arnā'ūṭ and Ḥusayn al-Asad. 25 vols. Beirut: Mu'assasa al-Risāla, 1981–1988.

Dols, Michael W., *Majnūn: The Madman in Medieval Islamic Society*. Oxford: Clarendon Press, 1992.

Elliott, Alison Goddard, *Roads to Paradise: Reading the Lives of the Early Saints*. Hanover, N.H. and London: University Press of New England, 1987.

Encyclopaedia of Islam, new ed. by H. A. R. Gibb. Leiden: E. J. Brill, 1960–2002.

Encyclopaedia Iranica, ed. Ehsan Yarshater. London: Routledge and Kegan Paul, 1985–continuing.

Encyclopaedia of the Qur'ān, ed. J. D. McAuliffe. Leiden: Brill, 2001–2006.

The Encyclopedia of Religion, ed. Mircea Eliade and C. J. Adams, New York: Macmillan, 1987.

Ernst, Carl W., *Rūzbihān Baqlī: Mysticism and the Rhetoric of Sainthood in Persian Sufism*. Richmond, U.K.: Curzon Press, 1996.

———, "RŪZBIHĀN," in *Encyclopaedia of Islam*, new ed., vol. VIII, Leiden: E. J. Brill, 1960–2002, 651–652.

———, "SHAṬḤ," in *Encyclopaedia of Islam*, new ed., vol. IX, Leiden: E. J. Brill, 1960–2002, 361–362.

———, *Words of Ecstasy in Sufism*. Albany: State University of New York Press, 1985.

Forman, Robert K. C., *Mysticism, Mind, Consciousness*. Albany: State University of New York Press, 1999.

Frank, Tamar, "'Taṣawwuf is . . .': On a Type of Mystical Aphorism," *Journal of the American Oriental Society* 104 (1984): 73–80.

Gilliot, Cl., "ṬABAḲĀT," in *Encyclopaedia of Islam*, new ed., vol. X, Leiden: E. J. Brill, 1960–2002, 7–10.

Gramlich, Richard, *Alte Vorbilder des Sufitums: Erster Teil: Scheiche des Westens*. Wiesbaden: Harrassowitz Verlag, 1995.

———, *Schlaglichter über das Sufitum: Abū Naṣr as-Sarrāǧs Kitāb al-lumaʿ eingeleitet, übersetzt und kommentiert*. Stuttgart: Franz Steiner Verlag, 1990.

Halm, H., "al-ḲUSHAYRĪ," in *Encyclopaedia of Islam*, new ed., vol. V, Leiden: E. J. Brill, 1960–2002, 526–527.

Hamad, Bushra, "History and Biography," *Arabica* 45 (1998): 215–232.

The Holy Qur-an: Text, Translation and Commentary by Abdullah Yusuf Ali. Lahore: Sh. Muhammad Ashraf, 1938 (repr. 1977).

Homerin, Th. Emil, "'Tangled Words': Towards a Stylistics of Arabic Mystical Verse," in *Reorientations/Arabic and Persian Poetry*, ed. Suzanne P. Stetkevych. Bloomington and Indianapolis: Indiana University Press, 1994, 190–198.

Hosain, Hidayet [and H. Massé], "HUDJWĪRĪ," in *Encyclopaedia of Islam*, new ed., vol. III, Leiden: E. J. Brill, 1960–2002, 546.

Huart, Cl., [and H. Massé], article 'DJĀMĪ' in *Encyclopaedia of Islam*, new ed., vol. II, Leiden: E. J. Brill, 1960–2002, 421–422.

al-Hujwīrī, ʿAlī Ibn ʿUthmān al-Jullābī, *Kashf al-maḥjūb*, ed. V. Zhukovski. Tehran: Amīr Kabīr, 1336 a.h.s. (repr.)

———, *The Kashf al-Maḥjūb*, translated by R. A. Nicholson. Leiden: E. J. Brill and London: Luzac and Co., 1911 (repr. Lahore: Islamic Book Foundation, 1982).

Humphreys, R. Stephen, *Islamic History: A Framework for Inquiry*. Rev. ed. Princeton, N.J.: Princeton University Press, 1991.

Hurvitz, Nimrod, "Biographies and Mild Asceticism: A Study of Islamic Moral Imagination," *Studia Islamica* 85 (1997): 41–65.

Ibn Khallikan's Biographical Dictionary, trans. Bn Mac Guckin de Slane. 4 vols. Beirut: Librairie du Liban, 1970 repr.

al-Iṣfahānī, Abū Nu'aym, *Ḥilyat al-awliyā' wa-ṭabaqāt al-aṣfiyā'*, ed. Muṣṭafā 'Abd al-Qādir 'Aṭā. 10 vols. Beirut: Dār al-Kutub al-'Ilmīya, 1988, repr.

Jāmī, 'Abd al-Raḥmān Ibn Aḥmad, *Nafaḥāt al-uns min ḥaḍarāt al-quds*, ed. Mahdī Tawḥīdī Pūr. Tehran: Intishārāt 'Ilmī, 1375 a.h.s.

al-Kalābādhī, Abū Bakr Muḥammad Ibn Isḥāq, *al-Ta'arruf li-madhhab ahl al-taṣawwuf*, ed. 'Abd al-Ḥalīm Maḥmūd. Cairo: Maktaba al-Thaqāfa al-Ḥīnīya, n.d.

———, *The Doctrine of the Ṣūfis*, translated by A. J. Arberry. Lahore: Sh. Muhammad Ashraf, 1966 repr.

Karamustafa, Ahmet T., *Sufism: The Formative Period*. Edinburgh: Edinburgh University Press, 2007.

Kennedy, Hugh, *When Baghdad Ruled the Muslim World: The Rise and Fall of Islam's Greatest Dynasty*. Cambridge, Mass.: Da Capo Press, 2004.

Khairallah, As'ad E., *Love, Madness, and Poetry: An Interpretation of the Maǧnūn Legend*. Beirut: Orient-Institut der Deutschen Morgenländischen Gesellschaft, 1980.

Khalidi, Tarif, *Arabic Historical Thought in the Classical Period*. Cambridge, U.K.: Cambridge University Press, 1994.

———, "Islamic Biographical Dictionaries: A Preliminary Assessment," *Muslim World* 63 (1973): 53–65.

al-Khaṭīb al-Baghdādī, Abū Bakr Aḥmad Ibn 'Alī, *Ta'rīkh Baghdād*, ed. Muṣṭafā 'Abd al-Qādir 'Aṭā. 24 vols. Beirut: Dar al-Kutub al-'Ilmīya, 1997 repr.

Khoury, Raif G., "Importance et authenticité des texts de *Ḥilyat al-awliyā' wa-ṭabaqat al-aṣfiyā'* d'Abū Nu'aym al-Iṣbahānī," *Studia Islamica* 46 (1977): 73–113.

Kinberg, Leah, "The Legitimization of the *Madhāhib* Through Dreams," *Arabica* 32 (1985): 47–79.

Knysh, Alexander, *Islamic Mysticism: A Short History*. Leiden: Brill, 2000.

———, "Ṣūfism and the Qur'ān," in *Encyclopaedia of the Qur'ān*, vol. V, Leiden: E. J. Brill, 2001–2006, 137–159.

The Koran Interpreted, translated by A. J. Arberry. Oxford: Oxford University Press, 1964 (repr. 1991).

Lane, Edward William, *An Arabic-English Lexicon*. 2 vols. Cambridge, U.K.: Islamic Texts Society Trust, 1984 (repr.).

Lapidus, Ira M., *A History of Islamic Societies*. Cambridge, U.K.: Cambridge University Press, 2nd ed., 2002.

Lewisohn, Leonard, and Shackle, Christopher (eds.), *'Aṭṭār and the Persian Sufi Tradition: The Art of Spiritual Flight*. London, New York: I. B. Tauris and the Institute of Ismaili Studies, 2006.

Lings, Martin, "Mystical Poetry," in *The Cambridge History of Arabic Literature: 'Abbasid Belles-Lettres*, ed. Julia Ashtiany, T. M. Johnstone, J. D. Latham, R. B. Serjeant and G. R. Smith. Cambridge, U.K.: Cambridge University Press, 1990,235–264.

———, *Sufi Poems: A Mediaeval Anthology*. Cambridge, U.K.: Islamic Texts Society, 2004.

Lory, P., "al-Sarrādj," *Encyclopaedia of Islam*, new ed., vol. IX, Leiden: E. J. Brill, 1960–2002, 65–66.

Losensky, Paul, "Words and Deeds: Message and Structure in ʿAṭṭār's *Tadhkirat al-awliyāʾ*," in *ʿAṭṭār and the Persian Sufi Tradition*, ed. Lewisohn and Shackle, 2006, 75–92.

Madelung, W., "ʿAbū Noʿaym al-Eṣfahānī," in *Encyclopaedia Iranica*, vol. I, London: Routledge and Kegan Paul, 1985, 354–355.

Makdisi, George, "Ṭabaqāt-Biography: Law and Orthodoxy in Classical Islam," *Islamic Studies* 32 (1993): 371–396.

Malti-Douglas, Fedwa, "Controversy and Its Effects in the Biographical Tradition of al-Khatīb al-Baghdādī," *Studia Islamica* 46 (1977) 115–131.

———, "Dreams, the Blind, and the Semiotics of the Biographical Notice," *Studia Islamica* 51 (1980): 137–162.

Massignon, Louis, *The Passion of al-Hallāj, Mystic and Martyr of Islam*, translated by Herbert Mason. 4 vols. Princeton, N.J.: Princeton University Press, 1982.

———, idem, abridged edition, translated and edited by Herbert Mason. Princeton, N.J.: Princeton University Press, 1994.

Melchert, Christopher, "The Ḥanābila and the Early Sufis," *Arabica* 48 (2001): 352–367.

———, "The Transition from Asceticism to Mysticism at the Middle of the Ninth Century C.E.," *Studia Islamica* 83 (1996): 51–70.

Mojaddedi, Jawid A., *The Biographical Tradition in Sufism: The* Ṭabaqāt *Genre from al-Sulamī to Jāmī*. Richmond, U.K.: Curzon Press, 2001.

———, "Legitimizing Sufism in al-Qushayri's *Risala*," *Studia Islamica* 90 (2000): 37–50.

Nwyia, Paul, *Exégèse coranique et langage mystique*, 2nd ed. Beirut: Dar el-Machreq Sarl, 1991.

Ormsby, Eric L., "The Taste of Truth: The Structure of Experience in al-Ghazālī's *al-Munqidh min al-Ḍalāl*" in *Islamic Studies Presented to Charles J. Adams*, ed. Wael B. Hallaq and Donald P. Little. Leiden: E. J. Brill, 1991, 133–152.

Pazouki, Shahram, "Sufi Saints and Sainthood in ʿAṭṭār's Tadhkirat al-awliyā,'" in *ʿAṭṭār and the Persian Sufi Tradition*, ed. Lewisohn and Shackle. London and New York: I. B. Tauris and the Institute of Ismaili Studies, 2006, 63–74.

Pedersen, J., "ABŪ NUʿAYM al-IṢFAHĀNĪ," in *Encyclopaedia of Islam*, new ed., vol. I., Leiden: E. J. Brill, 1960–2002, 142–143.

The Qurʾan: A New Translation by M. A. S. Abdel Haleem. Oxford: Oxford University Press, 2004.

al-Qushayrī, ʿAbd al-Karīm Ibn Hawāzin, *Principles of Sufism*, translated by B. R. von Schlegell. Oneonta, N.Y.: Mizan Press, 1990.

———, *al-Risālat al-Qushayrīya fī ʿilm al-taṣawwuf*, ed. Maʿruf Zarīq and ʿAlī Balṭajī. Beirut: Dār al-Jīl, n.d.

Ravān Farhādi, A. G., *ʿAbdullāh Anṣārī of Herat (1006–1089 CE): An Early Ṣūfī Master*. Richmond, U.K.: Curzon Press, 1996.

Renard, John, *Friends of God: Islamic Images of Piety, Commitment and Servanthood*. Berkeley: University of California Press, 2008.

— (translator), *Knowledge of God in Classical Sufism: Foundations of Islamic Mystical Theology*. Mahwah, N.J.: Paulist Press, 2004.

Ritter, Hellmut, article "ʿAṬṬĀR," in *Encyclopaedia of Islam*, new ed., vol. I, 752–755.

Robinson, Chase F., *Islamic Historiography*. Cambridge, U.K.: Cambridge University Press, 2003.

———, "Prophecy and Holy Men in Early Islam," in *The Cult of Saints in Late Antiquity and the Early Middle Ages*, ed. James Howard-Johnston and Paul A. Hayward. Oxford: Oxford University Press, 1999, 241–262.

———, "The Study of Islamic Historiography: A Progress Report," in *Journal of the Royal Asiatic Society* series 3, 7 (1997): 199–227.

Sands, Kristin Zahra, *Ṣūfī Commentaries on the Qurʾān in Classical Islam*. Abingdon, U.K. and New York: Routledge, 2006.

al-Sarrāj al-Ṭūsī, Abū Naṣr ʿAbdallah b. ʿAlī, *The Kitāb al-Lumaʿ fi ʾl-Taṣawwuf*, ed. R. A. Nicholson. London: Luzac and Co, 1914 (1963 repr.).

Schimmel, Annemarie, *As Through a Veil: Mystical Poetry in Islam*. Oxford: Oneworld, 2001.

———, *Mystical Dimensions of Islam*. Chapel Hill: University of North Carolina Press, 1975.

Sellheim, R., "al-KHAṬĪB al-BAGHDĀDĪ," in *Encyclopaedia of Islam*, new ed., vol. IV, Leiden: E. J. Brill, 1960–2002, 1111–1112.

Sells, Michael A. (translator and ed.), *Early Islamic Mysticism: Sufi, Qurʾan, Miʿraj, Poetic and Theological Writings*. Mahwah, N.J.: Paulist Press, 1996.

al-Shiblī, Abū Bakr, *Dīwān*, ed. Kāmil Muṣṭafā al-Shaybī. Baghdad: Tabaʿ al-Ghalāf bi-Maṭbaʿat al-Biyān, 1967.

Shorter Encyclopaedia of Islam, ed. H. A. R. Gibb and J. H. Kramers. Leiden: E. J. Brill, 1953 (1974 repr.).

Sobieroj, Florian, "Love in the Mystical Discourse and Experience of Abū Bakr Shiblī," in *Sufi* 23, 1994, 10–15.

———, article "al-SHIBLĪ," in *Encyclopaedia of Islam*, new ed., vol. IX, Leiden: E. J. Brill, 1960–2002, 432–433.

Steingass, Franz, *Persian-English Dictionary*. London: Routledge and Kegan Paul, 1892 (1977 repr.).

Stroumsa, Guy G., "Madness and Divinization in Early Christian Monasticism," in *Self and Self-Transformation in the History of*

Religions, ed. David Shulman and Guy G. Stroumsa. New York: Oxford University Press, 2002, 73–88.

al-Sulamī, Abū ʿAbd al-Raḥmān, *Ḥaqāʾiq al-tafsīr*, ed. Sayyid ʿImrān. Beirut: Dār al-Kutub al-ʿIlmīya, 2001.

———, *Kitāb Ṭabaqāt al-Ṣūfiyya, Texte arabe avec une introduction* . . . par Johannes Pedersen. Leiden: E. J. Brill, 1960.

———, *Ṭabaqāt al-Ṣūfīya*, ed. Nūr al-Dīn Sharība, 2nd ed., Cairo: Maktaba ʾl-Khānjī, 1969.

Sviri, Sara, "The Self and Its Transformation in Sūfīsm, With Special Reference to Early Literature," in *Self and Self-Transformation in the History of Religions*, ed. David Shulman and Guy G. Stroumsa. New York: Oxford University Press, 2002, 195–215.

Wāyqānī, Kāẓam Muḥammadī, *Shibli: The Sane Mad-Man Islamic Jurist, Muhaddith, Gnostic and Sufi* (861–946 CE). Tehran: Kitāb-khāna Millī Irān, 1382 a.h.s.

Index